raising antiracist children

raising antiracist children

A PRACTICAL PARENTING GUIDE

Britt Hawthorne

with Natasha Yglesias

simon element

new york   london   toronto   sydney   new delhi

We dedicate this book to the antiracists who came before us,
the antiracists who resist alongside us,
and all the antiracists to come.

contents

authors' note

When writing this book, we relied upon our antiracist child-rearing communities, personal experiences, our memories, and our stories. To preserve the anonymity of certain individuals, we've modified identifying information of anyone who is not a close friend or family member.

We acknowledge that the specifics and dynamics of oppression, community, and language are constantly changing. When deciding on using certain terms in the book, we based our decision on contemporary acceptance of the terms at the time of writing, our education about the topics at hand, and our intuition. We recognize that we're always learning, and that some of these terms will change post-publication as conversations evolve and resistance transforms.

Lastly, we want to define what we mean by *parent*. We recognize that families come in many forms, and we intend for the word *parent* to be inclusive of the many types of caregivers in addition to society's traditional understanding of parents: grandparents, godparents, aunts, uncles, stepparents, cousins, siblings, and chosen parents or family, to name a few. When we use the words *parent* or *caregiver* in this book, we mean to include anyone who has a hand in raising the next generation.

a note to parents

Welcome! By reading this book, you're joining a community working to reimagine how homes will become liberated spaces. We want you to know that it's never too early to start creating a home rooted in justice, compassion, and love. So whether you're expecting or a seasoned caregiver, this book is for your family. Together, we'll practice empowered parenting by modeling, discussing, and taking action. Before you know it, your children will naturally take to anti-biased and antiracist (ABAR) ideals.

Our goal is to take the overwhelming feelings many parents have shared—anxiety about where to start and who to trust, as well as despair, helplessness, and hopelessness—away. Your goal will be to focus on becoming more comfortable and confident discussing racism, prejudice, and oppression with your family without the guilt and shame involved in these conversations, and to create everyday experiences that promote love and justice. Your awareness and examination will help your family take collective action against everyday and systemic injustices.

I'm Britt, and as a nationally recognized anti-bias and antiracist facilitator, I partner with action-orientated educators to create classroom environments that are inclusive and equitable for all learners.

But as a momma, I felt alone and unseen. Parenting books never quite affirmed who I was becoming as a mother and who I wanted my children to become. Sure, I wanted my children to become independent thinkers and doers, and I wanted them to develop a love of reading and playing outside. I wanted them to enjoy themselves. But I *also* wanted children who welcomed people, set healthy boundaries with their friends, discussed consent with their partners, knew how to rebel against injustice, and above all, children who deeply loved their neighbors. I wanted them to enjoy life and all of its diversity. Many of the parenting books out there focus on individualism—in this book, I'm looking to focus on collectivism. If I've learned anything, it's that alone we know a little, but together we know a lot. This work doesn't belong to any one person or group, it's everyone's work to do together.

This book will share some of the ways I've unknowingly upheld white dominant culture inside my home, but it'll also share our favorite toys and materials my family uses to practice accurate language, the critical conversations I'm holding with my children, and even how I select books for my home collection. This book is a collection of my experience as a classroom educator, an anti-bias and antiracist teacher-educator, and my life experience of being a momma in the margins. We invite you to share what resonates with you and activates your brain with your loved ones. We invite you to share your journey of learning and unlearning with your loved ones, too.

As you engage with this book, I ask you to commit to and model radical self-love, collective care, and community solidarity. **Radical self-love** is taking care of yourself, such as drinking water, responding with curiosity, and taking deep breaths—especially when feeling troubled or challenged. We can practice this right now, as you read these words. Go ahead: take three deep breaths.

Taking care of ourselves also means allowing ourselves to grow into who we wish to become. It's easier said than done. Defensiveness, denial, and judgment are easier to choose than reflection, humility, and patience. Allow the truth to take up space. When you find yourself learning from someone, receive the truth as a gift and have a gratitude statement ready: "Thank you so much for giving me the gift of truth so I can continue to grow. I appreciate you." You might also respond with "Thank you for taking care of me. I have the ability to change my behavior, and I will."

As we're taking care of ourselves, we must also take care of each other. **Collective care** means we're responsible for one another. We have a responsibility to hear the truth from others and to share the truth with others—that includes our children. Silence and complacency won't create the homes we're hoping for. If critical conversations seem daunting, you'll find a few strategies in Part Five (page 195) that can help set you in the right direction.

Collective care also means creating space for conversations to happen, sharing resources, and making yourself available to support your loved ones and your antiracist community at large.

Lastly, **community solidarity**: We work to center people of the global majority (I'll go into this term later), to cite our sources, and to work toward justice. As an act of solidarity, I'm working to reposition the parenting conversation to include more voices. Together with my cowriter, Tasha, I've invited fellow parents and caregivers of the global majority to share their antiracist journey with us. We all need more contemporary examples of everyday families taking antiracist action. When your learning leaves these pages, we ask you to cite the writers and sources shared in this book.

One final note: Antiracism belongs to those who choose it. It isn't a destination, it's a lifelong path. Action, dedication, and community are required to become an antiracist family. By choosing to create our own paths, we'll find other families seeking to create brave spaces of their own, a community to hold us accountable and to laugh out loud while doing it.

We're Rooting for You,

Britt and Tasha

introduction

In the spring of 2017, our four-year-old woke up one morning for school and said, "Mommy, Ms. Garcia told me to shut up." I was shocked; I didn't want to believe another teacher, especially a coworker of mine, could speak to a child that way. I asked him to tell me more. He put one of his stuffed animals on his bed, then pretended to be Ms. Garcia. He whispered: "Cobe, I need you to shut up." As I rubbed his back and thanked him for reporting it to me, I knew there would need to be radical change.

This kind of "everyday" educational aggression isn't uncommon for Black children, or even the worst kind of aggression they face. Black children have experienced far worse educational racism, resulting in Black learners being suspended at four times the rate of white learners nationally.[1] Indigenous, Black, and brown children continue to experience curricular violence and appropriation in textbooks, theatrical plays, class read-alouds, and holiday celebrations. This is what our children are up against, and it's called the **school-prison nexus.**

Families of the global majority still have to push for their schools to address racism, even when their students and teachers experience it daily. Racism is a part of everyday life here in the United States. **Critical Race Theory** is an academic and legal theory that's been around since the 1990s. This theory (which we agree with) states that racism doesn't happen only on an interpersonal level but also on a systemic level. It challenges the notion that racist attacks are unfortunate and rare, that they happen only to a few people, and that the attackers will always make it clear they're perpetrating a hate crime. Instead, critical race theory gives legal students, lawyers, and academic scholars a framework to analyze how racism is baked into policies, laws, and the legal and punishment system. CRT is not being taught in K–12 classrooms; it's an academic and theoretical framework specifically for those in the legal field.

However, the very idea of critical race theory—and antiracism—is under attack. This attack is part of a larger historical pattern of white rage and white backlash. Currently, it's against the Black Lives Matter movement's progress. Antiracism—not to be confused with CRT—offers people the chance to analyze racism on a deeper, more accessible, and systemic level.

We now have more people who understand that success occurs not simply because of personal responsibility and hard work but also because of power, immunity, and oppression. There are more educators equipped with the tools, resources, training, and desire to teach a more truthful and accurate history. But what happens when you have educators who are not only resistant but emboldened in their ignorance by state-sponsored policies to not address racism in the classroom, even when it's occurring right in front of them?

After school, the four of us—Ms. Garcia; the two lead teachers, Ms. Lacey and Ms. Jess; and I—stumbled through a critical conversation. Ms. Garcia admitted to telling Cobe to shut up after trying and failing to get him to be quiet during nap time multiple times. Apparently, her frustration got the best of her. Ms. Lacey, Ms. Jess, and I all made it crystal clear that educators never tell a student to shut up—no matter how frustrated we get—and that it's perfectly normal for a four-year-old to talk a lot. It was something that should've been a given. When Ms. Jess offered possible solutions like bringing Cobe to the kindergarten reading group, taking him to another classroom to work, walking the hallways, or letting him quietly color on his nap map, we learned that Ms. Garcia had in fact used these solutions for other talkative children, just not for Cobe in this situation. As an anti-bias and antiracist guide, my mind always buzzes with the "characters" in the story and the role we all play, so I asked, "If Cobe was talking, who was he talking to?"

"Noah," she replied. Noah was Cobe's best friend at the time: a blond-haired boy from France who was a year older than him.

"Did you also tell Noah to shut up?" I asked. Ms. Garcia looked me straight in the eyes and said, "No."

When we allow ourselves to think about how young children develop bias, learn prejudice, and treat others unfairly, we must think about the bias and prejudice they *experience* and *witness*. What example did Ms. Garcia set when she treated these children differently? How do young children begin to inaccurately rationalize these experiences, and how does this make them feel about their own identities?

My experience as a Black-Biracial mother, teacher, and justice educator was too exhausted to overanalyze this situation. This was not the first time my children faced prejudice in the classroom, and I knew that it unfortunately wouldn't be the last. How many more times would I have to tell educators to treat my children with dignity and respect? How many times would I wonder if my children are being treated unfairly? Would I continue to watch them normalize these experiences?

That moment with Ms. Garcia was the last straw. I decided then to make a radical choice for our family: we'd remove our children from the classroom and homeschool them. In 2017, I joined thousands of Black homeschoolers who also chose to resist the anti-Blackness deeply embedded in schools.[2] It's one thing to intellectualize white supremacy; it's another to experience what supremacy takes and takes and takes. This change took Cobe and his brother, Carter, out of their beloved school and away from their friends and community. It also took my classroom from me and took me away from my cherished learners and their families. It was hard for us all, but necessary for our well-being.

White supremacy isn't some abstract idea; it has real life-affecting consequences. Because of white supremacy, Indigenous, Black, brown, trans, queer, and disabled children of color are receiving unfair treatment. Because of white supremacy, white children are missing out on loving friendship, joyous experiences, and fully connecting to their humanity due to their developing pre-prejudice. As adults, we have to reckon with our own biases and irrational fears in order to raise a new generation of conscious, inclusive children. We have to agree to help children embrace human differences, accurately identify unfairness, receive accountability as a gift, interrupt the harmful discriminatory practices they witness, imagine a future where Black lives matter, and practice infinite hope. I'm guessing that's exactly why you picked up this book. You've participated in conversations about race and racism and you're ready to take action as a family.

While you engage with this book, my goal is for you and your children to experience a balance of effort and ease. At times, your breath will flow effortlessly and the activities will be affirming. Other times, you'll feel challenged, uncomfortable, and downright resistant. Remember that every time you feel challenged, it's a place to grow.

Our ABAR parenting journey will be rooted in seven chosen values: **authenticity**, **curiosity**, **collaboration**, **accountability**, **becoming**, **empowerment**, and **candor**. (A breakdown of these terms can be found on pages 123–24.) We chose values that would directly disrupt harmful dominant beliefs, support critical thinking, and allow our children to live out values of justice. We'll be going into the values in depth later in the book.

This book will structure ABAR parenting into five sections about your children and their world: deepening our understandings, healthy bodies, radical minds, conscious consumption, and thriving communities. Each section is filled with key takeaways, common misconceptions, and terms. Each section will also contain practical age-appropriate activities to do with your children to help reinforce justice and accountability in your home. Some will be specifically for children of color, some will be for white children, and some will be for both.

Watch out for discussion questions and reflective prompts along the way. Some of the prompts are for you and your parenting partners, designed for the adults in your life to discuss and process big topics before discussing them with your children. It's not enough to do this work with just our children; we have to do this work ourselves. We have to be aware of when we're using our children to avoid this work with our own peers. So use these discussion topics to think about the moments in your life that you want to re-create for your children, both the inevitable moments and the preventable ones.

There will be discussion questions and reflective prompts for you and your children to do together, as well. If anyone is struggling with the words, allow silence to be welcomed in the conversation. No one needs to have all the words or answers. Feel empowered to say, "It's perfectly healthy to have processing time." Processing time allows folks to engage in rather than avoid a conversation. In our home, if our children need to process, we can do that in silence by utilizing trauma-informed movements, playing board games, writing notes back and forth, and doing art. If your children catch you off guard with a question and you need to process, model processing time by responding with one of my go-to phrases:

1. "We'll talk on Friday when I have more information," or
2. "What three questions do you have for me? I'll go research them," or
3. "Can you tell me what you already know?"

Just remember, as an anti-bias and antiracist caregiver, we never avoid a conversation because of our own discomfort.

All of the activities in this book are by invitation only; some will be applicable right away, while others are for you to recommend to your friends and family. Thank you for choosing us to guide you on this ABAR parenting journey.

deepening our understandings

In order to begin the work of anti-bias and antiracism, we must first identify our starting points of reference so we can know where we need to begin our educational journey. This section will be all about ensuring we're on the same page so you can move forward confident and informed. Remember: the point is not to talk *at* your child for these exercises and discussions. In order to achieve liberation and equality, we must partner *with* the next generation to create the future they deserve.

Where Do We Begin?

Cultivating liberation is a framework for families seeking social, political, and economic change. When engaging with the framework, one will feel a sense of responsibility and direction. We did not *create* the oppressive system, and yet we're always being advantaged or disadvantaged by that system, and we have the power to bring about different outcomes. The foundation of our liberation framework is **community**: we must cultivate the ability and capacity to deeply care for one another. When we're truly in and relating to our community, we'll sense the injustices and justices of the world. If we're lucky enough to have a strong community, its members will challenge us to take action, encourage us to listen more, and generously share their wisdom.

Our sense of community encourages us to plant seeds of curiosity and watch them grow. We're curious about our language, position, thoughts, ideas, and beliefs. We watch for the bias and injustice our children may encounter. Most important, we're curious about power: who has it, who's using it, and who's misusing it? The seeds of curiosity will grow into possibilities of change. What are your values, goals, and desired outcomes? What do you imagine happening instead? How much time do you have to commit, and what are your resources? Once we have a running list of choices, we're ready to create change with our community.

Creating change looks and feels different for each person. You might create change with your local parent-teacher organization, by preparing your home environment to affirm your children, by supporting someone else in creating change, by working with your family members to create change, or any combination of these. There's no one right way to create change. Laying the foundation for community helps us know we aren't doing this work alone. Our community cultivates liberation when we're curious about who we are and the systems we uphold, and when we consider different possibilities and commit to change.

An Antiracist Prepared Environment Is Imperative

Our home becomes our workspace to create an environment where children are affirmed, play with the language of justice, and embrace human diversity. We start by acknowledging that we live in a racist society and that we must challenge the racist messages, ideas, and actions our children encounter. We use books, toys, art supplies, puzzles, dolls, movies, podcasts, audiobooks, and other mediums as tools to center joy. Materials, prompts, and family discussions are used to think about power, the misuse of power, accountability, and agency.

Children Need Respect and Understanding

In an antiracist home, we build trusting relationships with our children. Instead of viewing our children as a problem to be solved, appreciate their mystery. Offer them respect and seek to understand them. We're not raising children for compliance and obedience. Our purpose as parents and caregivers is to raise children to be full participants in a democracy for liberation. This requires children to think critically, make choices, accept responsibility for their actions, and be empowered creatives. My friend Simone Davies beautifully explains how children as young as toddlers can practice this by having "the freedom of choice, movement, and will." This freedom (with limits) means our children have the right to choose what they'd like to wear, how much they want to eat, what they'll watch, and who they'll play with. It means trusting the environment you've prepared and your children to make choices for themselves. When mistakes happen, it also means moving away from a reward-and-punishment system and into a restorative practice.

Creating Your Own Practices

We don't need perfect antiracist parents, we need parents willing to practice antiracism with curiosity and commitment. As I've mentioned previously, antiracism isn't just something to read about or something to do at a set time of the day, it's a lifestyle. Moving forward, each section is filled with practices you can do with your child. As always with lists, we never want to limit our imagination, so feel empowered to create your own practices and share with your community. Here are a few things I kept in mind when creating my lists:

1. Use what I have.
2. Lead by example and model the attitudes, language, and actions I expect.
3. Go slow and steady with each concept, accepting we won't finish learning today.
4. Ask my community for support.
5. Spend time observing my children and listening to their stories.

What Does It Mean to Be an Antiracist Co-Conspirator?

For many of us, living in a racist society means we begin our accountability work as active allies. **Allies** spend their time thinking, analyzing, and understanding. Dr. Barbara J. Love's words sit with me when I think of this notion: "Asking what, if anything, needs to happen to move the reality that we are witnessing or experiencing on a path toward liberation, and what our role should be in that movement." An ally believes with their heart but doesn't live in harmony with their actions. Changing your profile picture to say "Black Lives Matter" or posting a black square on social media tells your community what you believe, but your actions (or lack thereof) do little to change the institutional and systemic injustices, allowing the status quo to thrive. Being a **co-conspirator** means you're willing to disrupt, build, and when necessary, dismantle for the future you want to have. You want to be able to say, "I'm an active participant working toward justice."

An **accomplice** in justice understands that Black, Indigenous, and people of color don't have the luxury to pause racial injustice, and so an accomplice doesn't, either. You move from ally to accomplice when you live in harmony with your beliefs and actions. bell hooks says,

"What we do is more important than what we say, or what we say we believe." An accomplice understands that this is a weight you must be willing to carry and never put down.

You know you're becoming a co-conspirator when those actions become a lifestyle. These are active verbs we're practicing and moving through—they're never static identities—so I prefer to preface each one with *becoming*. We acknowledge that we're not always and can't always be co-conspirators. Sometimes we're active allies because we're still learning, while other times we're accomplices. If this resonates with you, will you say the next three sentences with me?

I am becoming an active ally.
I am becoming an accomplice in justice.
I am becoming a co-conspirator.

What Is Bias?

All brains have bias. In the simplest terms, biases are preferences or shortcuts our brains take to process information we receive. Reducing bias is pretty demanding, because it's easier to see someone else's bias rather than our own. That's why having authentic relationships where people can share the gift of truth with us is necessary. We would never want to eliminate all of our biases, because it would mean starting every decision from zero. However, we do want to be aware of what biases negatively affect the way we connect with other human beings and the messages we're sending to our children. Otherwise, we could unintentionally commit **microaggressions**: swift, offhand remarks that reveal our prejudices, perpetuating discrimination and preventing us from being aligned with our values.

Let's focus on two biases—the ostrich effect and the affinity effect (or in-group bias)—that will help your family make better decisions. Have you ever seen a cartoon with an ostrich sticking its head in the sand? Even though ostriches don't actually do that, the imagery remains pretty powerful. The **ostrich effect** causes us to avoid the information we think will cause a negative emotional reaction. Humans are great at avoidance, either physically or mentally. We avoid the news, we let those bills pile up, we put off the dentist appointment, or telling a coworker that comment was rooted in racism, even when we know it's better to address the concern. Instead of being the ostrich, work to be the eagle. Looking at issues from up high helps you to see the bigger picture and find your place in the work.

When you're shopping and you need to ask a store associate a question, you're much more likely to seek someone who shares your racialized identity. This is known as the **affinity effect**, which thrives due to in-group bias. **In-group bias** is very common and unlike out-group—or unconscious—bias. Out-group bias says: I'm treating you unfairly because you're different or in the "out-group." In-group bias causes us to favor people who we perceive are like us. This can affect our decision-making about things like the school we choose, the pediatrician we choose, where we purchase a house, the accounts we follow on social media, the places we worship, the friendships we make, and even how we offer people grace in tough situations.

University of Toronto professor Kang Lee says two of his recent studies indicate that racial bias may "arise in babies as young as six to nine months of age." In the first study, Lee showed that six- to nine-month-old babies began to "associate faces from their own race with happy music and those from other races with sad music." In the second study, researchers found that "babies as young as six months were more inclined to learn information from an adult of his or her own race, rather than from an adult of a different race." These study findings point to the possibility that "racial bias may arise out of our lack of exposure to other-race individuals in infancy," Lee said.[1] This invites us to find ways we can intentionally expose our children to racial differences in the early months.

Expressing Boundaries and Requesting to Be Heard

When we first started our antiracist journey, my family and I used the courageous conversation agreements by Glenn E. Singleton and Curtis Linton. These four agreements are: **stay engaged, speak your truth, experience discomfort**, and **expect and accept non-closure**. These principles allow our family to practice fostering a curious and empathetic space. At first, I spent time thinking about each category and how it showed up in my relationships. Then I thought about the ways I shut down these agreements: the things that led me to disengage, stay silent, protect my own comfort, and expect closure in every situation. After that, I thought about how I could make these courageous conversation agreements practical and started making small commitments to myself before inviting my children into the activity.

If this is new for you, I suggest working with your parenting partners first and discussing what you'd like to model in everyday moments. Ask yourself: What are my agreements to myself and the community I'm accountable for? There isn't a right way; each person chooses what they need depending on how they disengage in conversations, project emotions, center their comfort, and look for quick fixes. These checkpoints will be imperative when you begin having necessary conversations on topics such as prejudice, accountability, or respect. When your children are ready to co-create accountability agreements, start by asking them:

1. "What will help you stay engaged in an activity or conversation?"
2. "How can you speak your truth even when it's difficult?"
3. "Learning is uncomfortable and sometimes being wrong feels heavy. How can you take care of yourself to keep learning?"
4. "It's easy to start and not finish; it's a commitment to finish something we started. What can we do to remember to keep going?"

5. "What would you like me to do when you are . . ."
6. "How can I support you to . . ."

Below, you can find examples of our children's agreements and how their agreements have changed over the years.

Topics	Age: 4 years old	Age: 8 years old	Age: 14 years old
Staying Engaged	"I need a hug."	"I need five minutes in my room."	"I need to move while talking."
Speaking Your Truth	"I" statements.	"Please don't take my turn."	"I need processing time to write my thoughts down."
Experiencing Discomfort	"Time for deep breaths."	"Sips of water would be helpful."	"Let's talk about it in the car."
Expecting and Accepting Non-Closure	"We can discuss it over lunch."	"I'll write it down in my notebook to ask again."	"I'll send a calendar invite to follow up."

Helping Children Maintain Boundaries

Boundary setting with children includes consent. In my household, we introduced the idea of consent at a very early age. We're moving beyond the binary of yes means yes or no means no: consent for us means a constant and collaborative conversation. Montessori director and toddler teacher Corey Jo Lloyd explains consent as "a constant conversation not just about who touches who, it's ultimately about shared power." For young children, this means they're in control of their bodies; if they want to hug, receive a kiss, have their picture taken, or wear a costume, they can actively consent to that. Each time we ask, our children have the right to make a choice for themselves, and we must honor that choice. As adolescents engage in romantic relationships, each partner has the right to choose if they want to hold hands, hug, kiss, be touched, or have sex. They have the right to make the same choice or a different choice for themselves, and their partners need to honor that choice.

Words really do matter. Here are some go-to assertive phrases I encourage and model for our children to use:

- If someone is tickling them: "Stop it!"
- If someone interrupts them: "I haven't finished my turn."
- If someone cuts in line for the slide: "You may go when I am done with my turn."
- If someone wants to come into the bathroom with them: "We have a safety rule."
- If someone makes fun of them: "We all get to be different."
- If someone goes to touch their body: "You don't have my permission."

When my children uphold their boundaries, I respond with these two phrases I picked up from Ashley Speed, a queer Montessori educator helping teachers and parents honor the fullness of children's identity and expression:

- Thank you for communicating your boundaries.
- Thank you for respecting your boundaries.

What Is Antiracism?

Antiracism is more than being *against* racism—it's actively being for freedom, liberation, and justice. Instead of viewing antiracism as a destination or a place to arrive, see it as a consistent, active practice: a lifestyle. As antiracists, we're consciously considering the possibilities of power, inequality, and our roles and responsibilities to take action. Antiracism is about understanding how racism functions in our home and committing to resist it. It's an active approach to repair historical and contemporary injustices. Being antiracist means we're choosing antiracist actions by making space for Indigenous, Black, brown, and people of color, voting to pass antiracist laws and policies that will mitigate harm caused to people of color, having open and honest conversations about race and racism with people, and creating a culture of unapologetic love and care. It's about imagining and building solidarity for Indigenous, Black, brown, and people of color in order for them to thrive.

When our homes are antiracist places, it allows each person to be valued, trusted, and accepted for who they are, who they're becoming, and who they'll be.

Here are five principles to keep in mind while parenting:

1. Community is at the heart of antiracism.
2. Children have a natural desire to learn.
3. Antiracism requires imagination, creativity, and action.
4. An antiracist-prepared environment is imperative.
5. Re-parenting is required; enjoy the learning and unlearning that will happen.

Community Is at the Heart of Antiracism

The Nigerian Igbo proverb "it takes a village to raise a child" resonates with me best. There's so much wisdom in this proverb because it challenges us to build and sustain the community our children need.

Our children require a village of antiracist humans. Let's break down what I mean when I say *community*. Your community can consist of blood relatives, friends, or chosen kinships. Your community is multigenerational, and diverse in thought, experiences, and physical representation. Your community is rooted in love. Everyone won't think exactly alike or even agree on how to be antiracist. It also doesn't mean everyone will get along or even like each other (shocking, I know!). Being a part of an antiracist community means you're an indispensable member of the community; our community is better simply by you being a part of it. Each person brings their special talents, gifts, and skills to our community and shares them. Our community is sharing in the work, inviting us to gatherings, rallies, and potlucks. Our community is organizing inclusive playdates, checking on one another, and sharing resources such as books, toys, clothes, and wisdom. Our community is rooting for each other to grow.

What Do We Mean by "Global Majority"?

We choose to use the term *people of global majority* (or PoGM, a term coined by Dr. Barbara J. Love) because it directly disrupts white supremacy. There are more people of color in this world than white people. Yet media, educational curricula, and pop culture continue to center white people. The term *people of the global majority* acts to challenge this myth. In the United States, PoGM have a shared history of being pushed out, denied access, made to feel perpetually othered and not American enough. White people, however, are seen as neutral; they're the assumed default, always centered in the conversation.

Black people, Indigenous people, brown people, Latine/x peoples—particularly Indigenous and Afro-Latine/x peoples—Pacific

Islanders, Native Hawaiians, the Inuit communities/Alaska Natives, Native Americans, Arabs, Western Asians/Middle Easterners with dark skin, North Africans, Southeast Asians, South Asians, East Asians, Africans with dark skin, and biracial and multiracial people who are mixed with one or more of the above, and people and groups who can't access white privilege are people of the global majority. This isn't a perfect definition. It's important to keep in mind that there are both white and non-white folks who hold different ethnicities that are also targeted by white domination. We acknowledge that this complicates the narrative that white domination works so hard to simplify.

Note: Lumping all of these groups together into one category can be a form of erasure. If you're discussing a particular group or groups, refer to the group by specific identity.

What Does It Mean to Think and Parent Intersectionality?

When referring to antiracism or racial justice work, we're working toward equal outcomes for all people. We center racism in the conversation because we understand racism is the undercurrent that leads to disproportionate outcomes, but we do not stop there. We focus on all justice while ensuring racism is being acknowledged and dismantled, not compartmentalized as a separate issue. As antiracists, we advocate for the justice of other identity groups because liberation should not be exclusionary or conditional. We must remember that Black and brown folks can be queer, trans, disabled, Muslim, Jewish, neurodivergent, and any number of other identities; there is no finite list.

In a speech to the National Women's Political Caucus in 1971, titled "Nobody's Free Until Everybody's Free," Fannie Lou Hamer famously said, "the changes we have to have in this country are going to be for liberation of all people—because nobody's free until everybody's free."

Parenting intersectionality means looking at your family's identity profile and noticing how your family's overlapping identities experience discrimination or receive advantages. It means accepting and embracing all aspects of your children so you don't unintentionally perpetuate the discrimination they experience elsewhere, and so that they know they have a safe space where they are fully accepted no matter what. As caregivers, it's important that we create safe spaces for the children in our lives that acknowledge, celebrate, and nurture all the parts of their identity, not just some. It also means we make sure to not assume our children's identity.

To create an identity profile for your family, take stock of the personal and group identities everyone holds and the social advantages and disadvantages you all experience.

1. **Personal identities**—the qualities that make each child unique. A few examples are hobbies, how they like to spend their time, their skills, what they are learning to accomplish and their talents, and what they can naturally do.
2. **Group identities**—characteristics they have in common with larger groups. A few examples are age, gender, ability and disability, worldview, and ethnicity.
3. **Social inequities**—the unfair discrimination people experience caused by institutions, organizations, policies, and laws.

For the children who hold multiple marginalized identities, their discrimination is often compounded by the specific juxtaposition of these identities, usually causing them to not feel wholly accepted or supported by one community of their identity profile or another. I'll create space for Tasha here to share her experience holding multiple identities:

My particular experience being queer and Latina often leaves me feeling at odds with myself. With my "traditional," more conservative Cuban family—which I love with all my heart—I still feel uncomfortable being openly queer. Most members know how I identify, but conversations about the intricacies of my dating life are either avoided or glossed over to avoid discomfort or awkwardness. I know my family loves and accepts me, but I can tell many of them feel uncomfortable or unprepared to have open conversations about my queerness.

Alternatively, in many designated queer spaces and queer events in the Bay Area, I often fail to see other Latine/x folks (and people of color in general) represented. The San Francisco queer scene seemed to focus on cisgender gay white men; when I entered those spaces, I felt very unwelcome. Luckily, I've had better luck finding more inclusive queer spaces in the East Bay, but it took a lot of time and trust to feel at home in those spaces, too.

I often feel as though I have to mute one aspect of myself in order to exist in the space of the other. Part of that is internalized pressure, and part of that is reinforced externalized pressure. For example, I received a lot of messages from my family both explicitly and implicitly that queerness was a touchy subject, a subject that was "nobody's business." That line of thinking has impacted my level of comfort and confidence in myself, and it's caused me to second-guess how open I should act when meeting new people, even in designated queer spaces. In queer spaces near where I live, I'm very aware of how my background and personal experience others me in different ways.

It's painful to feel othered in a space you're a part of. I want to have the best relationship possible with both my family and my friends, but it's difficult to navigate when I don't feel wholly embraced by either group. Part of my work moving forward is to trust and hope my communities accept me as I become more open and honest about who I am. Their work is to deliver on that hope.

—Tasha Yglesias

Unpacking the Story

- Who is missing from the conversation/representation? Who is being erased, othered, or silenced?
- Who is being centered? Who is being praised and affirmed?
- How are these two groups having similar experiences yet different outcomes?
- What absolute truths are being normalized in this conversation?
- What history is being forgotten?

Parenting intersectionality allows us to recenter conversations to include Black, brown, and/or Indigenous mothers from the global majority, working-class families, disabled parents, migrant families, immigrant families, fathers, and queer families, just to name a few. It would assert them as experts in their perspectives and spotlight their particular experience with joy and also discrimination.

We know people with nondominant identities are being compared to the expectations, values, and norms of the dominant identities, and this creates different discriminatory outcomes. Among the many cases of institutional discrimination, Deandre Arnold sticks out to me. He was a student at Barbers Hill High School, a public school in Mont Belvieu, Texas, not too far from Houston. He was suspended indefinitely because his hair was too long, just past his shoulders. He would not be allowed to be in the classroom until he cut his hair, even after his family explained it was long for cultural reasons. Deandre's hair challenged the dominant standard of men's hair length and the loc style conflicted with Eurocentric dominant standards of what is acceptable and expected. Intersectionality helps us ensure that we don't view Arnold as only a Black student or only as a male, instead realizing *both* are contributing to the discrimination he's experiencing. Intersectionality also helps us analyze how these discriminating actions will affect him.

White Supremacy and Its Effects

First things first: Let's get grounded and know some resistance might be coming with the next few sections. Rise to the challenge to keep unlearning and relearning.

White supremacy affects all children across all institutions and lifestyles. While people are becoming more comfortable with using the term *white supremacy* in everyday conversation, the concept is still relatively misunderstood. White supremacy is the idea holding different forms of racism together: internalized, interpersonal, institutional, and structural, as well as other forms of oppression such as colorism and Eurocentrism. White supremacy is the collusion of public and private institutions and their policies to benefit white people at the expense of everyone else. At the root, it's the misuse of power to hoard resources. White supremacy doesn't act alone; it's often intertwined with other oppressive ideologies like heteronormativity, the patriarchy, and neoliberalism. The biggest misconception is that white supremacy is loud and bold. I learned to associate only white supremacists, Ku Klux Klan members, and neo-Nazis with white supremacy, and this caused me to overlook the subtle aggressions that keep white supremacy ideology operating on a daily basis. White supremacy isn't one person or action, it's the ideology of whiteness being superior and about the concrete violence it enacts on people who don't get in line. It has been built over centuries, resulting in a well-oiled, normalized machine.

Because someone will ask, "But must we say white supremacy?" Cynthia Miller-Idriss, an American University professor, offers this response: "Language matters because it's a reflection of how seriously something gets taken."

Even using the words *white supremacy* continues the idea that white people can be supreme. Therefore, I prefer a more accurate term, **white domination**, to describe how it's being used to dominate land, cultures, languages, and people. Try using this term in your daily life and see how it resonates for you.

Responding with Truth

I've invited Dr. Kira Banks, one of my parenting partners, to share how she centers the truth when discussing racist experiences with her children.

Oppression tells us lies about who we are. These inaccurate messages are by-products of systemic racism and can get picked up, or appropriated, through interactions, media, and the education system. You might have heard it referred to as internalized racism. I prefer talking about these lies as something that can be picked up rather than something that's inside me, because it's easier to put something down than to extract it.

Appropriated Racial Oppression: The extent to which people of the global majority accept the dominant group's idea that people of the global majority are subordinate, inferior, and deficient.

Appropriated Racial Superiority: The extent to which white people accept their group's idea that white people are dominant, superior, and natural leaders.

Kids can understand these ideas as soon as they can understand the story. As young as preschool, they notice who's seen as good, bad, smart, nice, and naughty. They watch scenes unfold in living rooms, playrooms, classrooms, and on screens. It's important for us, as adults, to be proactive and counter these inaccurate messages.

One way we can interrupt the appropriation of these stories is by naming the myths and lies as they come up around us. We can notice, question, and challenge them together.

For example, one day my nine-year-old had a baseball game. His team had several Black and brown boys, and the other team was all white. After the game, one little white boy refused to high-five the Black and brown boys on our team. When talking with my son, I reminded him that some white people had picked up the idea that they were better than Black people. This little boy might have been taught that Black people were not worthy of his high-five. "That's a lie, and it's sad he learned that," I said. "His actions say nothing about you but a lot about the ideas he has picked up." Research supports the idea that helping kids understand racism can help them not personalize it. My son did not dwell on whether he deserved the discrimination. He understood it was the other boy's problem rather than accepting the burden of feeling inferior as a result of the discrimination.

Next time you notice a myth or lie that says one group is better or deficient simply because of their race, name it. It can be as simple as stating the myth and lie, "I noticed . . . That's not accurate," "Did you hear that . . . It's like they're saying being white is better or makes a person more deserving. That's not true." When we name the myths and lies of racism, we help them have less of a hold on us. We put them down. We stop appropriating them, which frees us from some of the personal baggage of racism. Being clear about how these myths and lies show up and resisting them can make coming together to do the bigger systems' work of dismantling racism a tad bit easier.

—Dr. Kira Banks

What Is White Immunity?

If PoGM experience racism, what do white people experience? The answer is **white immunity**. With this term, we're moving beyond individual "privileges" to analyze how whiteness operates on a systemic level and how it benefits generations creating inequitable outcomes. We can use white immunity to analyze whether we're preparing our children for the world of racial diversity and racial justice. Historically, whiteness has been used to gain access to resourced neighborhoods and well-funded schools, and to create the best possible outcomes for people who uphold whiteness. Whiteness is also weaponized to exclude, wound, and incite acts of violence against Black, Indigenous, and children of color. Please research Native Boarding Schools (1860s–1970s), 16th Street Baptist Church bombing (1963), and the documentary *Rosedale: The Way It Is* (1975) for examples.

To make it concrete, white immunity allows white people to have a positive relationship with health-care providers. White immunity allows them a positive relationship with the police. White immunity allows white children to attend schools with more experienced teachers, more funding, and more resources. White immunity hoards opportunities like advanced placement courses, gifted and talented programs, and dual-language and Montessori programs. White immunity turns drug epidemics like the opioid crisis into a national concern, rallying mental health experts, state and local financial resources, and rehabilitative programs to be utilized. White immunity is supporting healthier outcomes for white children from the very beginning at the expense of children of the global majority. As Dr. Nolan Cabrera says: "White immunity means that People of Color have not been historically, and are not contemporarily, guaranteed their rights, justice, and equitable social treatment; however, White people are because they have protection from this disparate treatment."[2]

What Is White-Passing and White-Presenting?

Presenting, in the context of race, means that a person of the global majority or who is conditionally white is perceived as white or white-adjacent and therefore receives the immunities and the benefits of whiteness. This can be a complicated thing for most individuals who present as white. Historically, people of color or of multiracial ancestry who were white-presenting had the benefit of assimilation and safety in order to escape legal and social discrimination. For example, there were a small number of Jewish people in Nazi Germany who could present and pass as "Aryan," and this active **passing** was a means of escaping persecution. This assimilation usually was accompanied by guilt and internal conflict.

To most, passing can be seen as a rejection of someone's racial identity, their family, their history, and their culture, especially by the non-passing members of those communities. Presenting can also cause friction that leads to gatekeeping and exclusion, where some people of the global majority or who are conditionally white are disregarded by members of their own communities for seeming "too white." And the reverse can happen: some folks who present as white will gatekeep or exclude members of their communities.

Presenting and passing are complicated subjects, and many individuals (including those who do or do not present as white) have complicated feelings about it.

This is a perfect place to pause and discuss Jewish identity and antisemitism. As Liz Kleinrock points out, "Antisemitism is so often ignored, minimized, and justified. We must condemn antisemitism no matter where it comes from." I've invited Andy Lulka, one of my parenting partners, to briefly share about Jewishness, white supremacy, and antisemitism.

Jewishness, White Supremacy, and Antisemitism

Whenever discussions of antisemitism as a form of racial or ethnic discrimination rise to the forefront of social and political discourse, "Are Jews a race?" is a follow-up question that's usually posed. Anytime this question is asked, the Jewish people are in danger of being defined and viewed incorrectly by a world that has time and again persecuted us based on its own shifting definitions and categories that flatten our experience. This is especially true when it is white supremacists defining our nature.

The white supremacist extremist obsession with racial hygiene and racial purity as being related to moral, intellectual, and physical superiority forces humans with complex intersecting identities into broad categories that are organized hierarchically. Jewishness is very hard to categorize because our existence predates the categories used. This makes our very existence a threat to white domination. As much as we would like to think otherwise, white supremacist extremist belief systems are not actually separate from white-dominant culture—they support each other, feed each other, legitimize each other.

Broadly speaking, the end goals of most white supremacists are the eradication of Jewish people; the enslavement of Black people; the subjugation of all other people of the global majority; the conversion or eradication of all non-Christian religions (the kinds of Christianity that are acceptable shift historically and culturally); the elimination of impurities, including any kind of miscegenation, queerness, and disability through corrective measures or sterilization; and the relegation of white women to the role of incubators for the white race. Antisemitism is a lynchpin in white supremacist belief systems, and because it manifests differently from other forms of hate, it often goes unnoticed until mass violence erupts seemingly out of nowhere.

At the Charlottesville Unite the Right Rally, many people watching in horror were confused by the cry "Jews will not replace us." The greatest fear of white supremacists is losing white dominance. This fear goes by many names, including white genocide, the great replacement, and the new world order. This fear of losing dominance was behind most of the mass murders targeting women, immigrants, and racialized people, as well as the violence aimed at mosques and synagogues, globally in the last several years. Because white supremacists believe people of the global majority to be inferior, they cannot fathom how they could possibly be able to defeat white men. When they see their dominance waning, they pick up on an old myth that

Jews are simultaneously superhuman and subhuman and cast us in the role of puppet master, pulling the strings to create a takeover.

These are the myths, fears, and beliefs in which European and North American history are steeped. They're alive and well today in many groups that espouse them openly, and in others that use more coded language. Many marginalized people and communities have internalized some or all of these beliefs, about us or about other groups, because that is what a white-dominant society trains us to do.

Practicing antiracism and parenting intersectionality means looking at how these belief systems have taken root in society—as well as in our own hearts and minds—and doing what we can to challenge and uproot them. Our liberation is tied together. We will get farther if we understand how and why that is.

My commitment to antiracism stems from my Jewishness, as well as from my Montessori upbringing. In one of our texts, it is written "You are not obligated to complete the work, but neither are you free to abandon it."[3] It is unlikely that our generation of parents will end all forms of hate and white domination. There is, however, quite a lot we *can* do, especially together.

—Andy Lulka

Color Blindness Is a Misconception

> Be proud of our heritage. I want to get the language so right that everybody here will cry out, "YES! I'M BLACK. I'M PROUD OF IT. I'M BLACK AND BEAUTIFUL!"
>
> —Dr. Martin Luther King, Jr.

Color blindness is an ideology that presumes ignoring or disregarding someone's race, culture, or ethnicity is the way to end discrimination and therefore the correct way to interact with people of a different racial group.

In my parenting workshops, many caregivers proudly proclaim their child doesn't see color. To say young children don't see color is not only dismissive of their curious minds, but it also shows the adults' discomfort with discussing race. They presume seeing a person's skin color as a racist act. Typically, people who subscribe to this ideology believe they live in a postracial world and that racism isn't really a big deal anymore, or that they're creating racism by merely acknowledging racial identities in the first place. When people who subscribe to this ideology get challenged about racist behavior or thought patterns, they might respond with: "I'm not racist; I don't see color." What this response really shows is that color blindness is often used as a means of avoiding the discussion of discrimination, or the responsibility of accountability and repair.

There are several problems with this kind of statement:

1. We're all raised to think and feel certain ways about certain races. No one escapes bias; whether taught to us by our family, society, or friends, bias is instilled in us from a very young age.

2. Despite what you claim you don't notice, you're still granted privileges and immunity others are not. The inequities and dynamics of discrimination are still at play.

3. Ignoring a key part of who a person is doesn't make them feel respected, accepted, or understood. It ignores their history, their culture, and their experiences.

At birth, babies look equally at faces of all races. At three months, babies look more at faces that match the race of their caregivers.[4] Young children love sorting colors. Educators often ask young learners to sort the crayons, match the shapes by color, or to "tell me the color of the block." When I have the opportunity to meet young children, seeing children also see my skin tone. When children see a person's brown skin tone, it allows them to acknowledge another part of the humanity they're proud of. When young children ask about skin tone, I know their minds are turning, that they're really wondering, "Who am I and who am I not?" This natural curiosity needs to be embraced, not shut down.

Using the term is an excuse to avoid the hard work of unlearning and relearning history and to avoid acknowledging the discrimination communities face, so the goal will never be to become "color-blind." The goal will always be to embrace brown and black skin tones, to develop friendships regardless of race, and to work toward justice—this is what antiracism looks like.

Questions for parenting partners to consider:

1. As a child, how did your family contribute to the notion of color blindness?
2. At home, were racial differences acknowledged and discussed in positive ways?
3. Who were the adults in your life that helped you learn accurate language about racial differences?
4. What places (school, places of worship, etc.) openly acknowledged race?
5. How do you feel about discussing racial differences with your children today?

Cultural Appropriation versus Appreciation?

Culture is a pattern of behavior shared by a society, or group of people. Many different things make up a society's culture. These things include food, language, clothing, tools, music, arts, customs, beliefs, and

Appropriating cultures happens when we take pieces of a minoritized culture and use them out of context, change the meaning, diminish the significance altogether, and/or sell them for profit. Halloween stores are a perfect example of the process of cultural appropriation: stores sell cheap knockoffs for profit, and the people who purchase the costumes play dress-up for a fun temporary moment. It's imperative that we emphasize to children that cultures are not costumes. A child can take off a costume at the end of Halloween, but children of color can never take off their racial or cultural identity. Alicia Elliott wrote an article titled "Why Are Parents So Defensive About Play Teepees?" and there's one line from it that still resonates with me today: "Overcoming centuries of cultural appropriation may seem scary, but when you reframe your thinking to focus on respect and consent instead of immediate outrage, it all becomes much easier."[6] So can we all agree to practice cultural appreciation instead?

Cultural appreciation is when we have genuine cultural exchanges where each community is in charge of sharing their culture with the other. This builds relationships, prevents stereotypes, educates, and creates a welcoming space. Attending heritage museums and cultural festivals are two ways to directly support communities while enjoying and connecting with their different cultures, perspectives, and traditions. Cultural festivals and events in particular are great because the community extended an invitation to us to connect and learn. Any money made goes back to the communities putting on the events, as well.

How to Be a Co-Conspirator, From Race to Gender Identity and Beyond

As mentioned earlier, active allies—or beginners on their journey to being co-conspirators—are active participants working toward justice. Being an ally isn't who you are; it's not an identity or a destination, it's something you're doing. Focus more on the verb *being* than the noun *ally*. Allies spend time thinking about and analyzing problems and partaking in discussions, and most definitely possess a robust social justice vocabulary. These practices are necessary anytime we learn something new, but in racial justice it can become performative, even dangerous, when we stop our practice at allyship. Allyship is the first step, not the last.

Our goal is to move through the allyship stage of awareness by applying what we're learning to become accomplices. This will require vulnerability, humility, and patience. When we move from allyship to being an accomplice, we're moving from the "me" to the "we." Allies focus on their learning by centering themselves in the situation. Accomplices focus on relationships by centering harm or justice. As accomplices put their values and beliefs into action, they make it clear to all what they're about and what's accepted around them.

We can't stop there either; the goal will always be liberation. We also need to become co-conspirators—folks who are willing to risk it all in the name of justice. We know we're being co-conspirators when our beliefs and actions live in harmony.

With this in mind, here are steps you can take to begin being a co-conspirator. These are foundational, and not meant to be all-encompassing. Below, you'll also find an introduction into the Pyramid of Accountability, which details the nuances within the steps to transitioning from active ally to co-conspirator in visual form.

1. **Be Accountable**—You cannot be an active participant in racial justice until you fully acknowledge the ways in which you're racist, ableist, sexist (and any other -ism you perpetuate, either subconsciously or consciously). Saying that you aren't these things ignores the way society has raised you to subscribe to these ideologies. Recognize the ways you need to grow, admit to the ways you benefit from these systems being upheld, and continue to educate yourself so your actions are as informed as possible. Ignoring these truths to protect your ego places your feelings and comfort above the needs, experiences, and voices of marginalized people. Having frank conversations about how these ideologies have manifested in you with your children shows them you're self-aware and working toward self-liberation. It also allows them to be vigilant and let you know when they're witnessing that behavior in you. Witnessing you model this will teach them how to hold themselves accountable to change. Remember that in order to be accountable, we must be vulnerable and not defensive. Having these conversations de-centers shame we carry about our past (and our present) and instead recenters truth, commitment, and repair. Modeling this with your children is absolutely imperative.

2. **Dismantle and Rebuild**—Embed antiracist language and analysis in your current environments and systems. If you're a manager or an executive, use your immunity and influence to change hiring practices, trainings, company policies, and systems and processes to be more inclusive, equitable, and comprehensive. If you're a teacher or a professor, discuss and analyze white domination in the classroom. Examine the whitewashing of educational content with your students. Talk to your principals, presidents, deans, and the like to change admission processes, hiring practices, student and teacher handbooks, and community and educational policies. We must show children that dismantling white domination and implementing antiracist language and action is

necessary work both in our home life and professional life. That means looking to create spaces rooted in justice extends to their schools. Supporting the diversification and equitable funding of the public library, the public school system, and public green spaces for your children and all children is vital. Know that this process won't be a smooth one: you'll most likely encounter pushback, roadblocks, and criticism for trying to change the current systems in place. But revolution isn't easy, it's work.

3. **Defer and Refer**—Consistently defer to people whose identities are being marginalized so their voices and experiences can be heard and honored. Expanding who you're following on social media allows you to learn what people within a community are seeking. If you're asked a question about a community you don't represent, simply say, "I'm not qualified to answer that. But we can research it." Refer people of the global majority and other marginalized folks to opportunities, especially ones they typically wouldn't have access to. This also means giving up space so they can take up space. Model this for your children constantly so they can follow your example and make space for others.

4. **Disrupt**—Confront those in your environments that display racist, ableist, homophobic, transphobic, and sexist behavior (or any discriminatory behavior against an identity group). Stating "That doesn't align with our family values" explicitly shows to family members and your child what you will and won't allow. People of the global majority have been calling out bigoted behavior for generations, and it's not their work to do alone. If you're against racism, ableism, homophobia, transphobia, and sexism, you need to call it out, too. As a person with immunity and influence for at least one of these -isms, you have the ability to confront individuals and systems to advocate for better, more equitable treatment and policies. It's always okay to rock the boat when seeking justice, so we should normalize interrupting harm and disrupting the status quo no matter how uncomfortable it may be. Our children are listening and watching. If all we show them is silence, that's all they're going to know.

5. **Act and Fund**—Donate time, resources, space, and if possible, money to local organizations, causes, and groups that advocate for equity and repair. Show up when people ask you to. Take risks for the sake of justice.

Antiracism will never be boiled down to a checklist or a set of universal steps. We can give you the framework, but you'll need to do your own work and research to actualize these goals yourself.

The Pyramid of Accountability

PYRAMiD of ACCOUNTABiLity

Co-conspirator

Accomplice

Active Ally

Let's look further into the evolution of active ally to accomplice to co-conspirator with the visual aid of the Pyramid of Accountability. This pyramid breaks down the nuances between these three terms to highlight the difference in proactiveness.

PYRAMiD of ACCOUNTABiLity

In the Active Ally base, there are the following acts:

1. Amplify people of marginalized identities
2. Educate oneself
3. Share other people's stories
4. Comfortably redistribute resources
5. Experience minimal discomfort
6. Take reactive actions
7. Know the language
8. Identify stereotypes
9. Listen to teach others
10. Vote for antiracist/anti-bias policies
11. Prioritize voices of the global majority

In the middle Accomplice tier, these are the following associated acts:

1. Be proactive
2. Share their personal stories
3. Recommend or recruit others in the work
4. Interrupt harmful jokes/comments
5. Challenge stereotypes
6. Understand the privileges and immunities they receive
7. Make space
8. "Hold the door open"
9. Change your behaviors
10. Establish just policies and values
11. Advocate for training and professional development
12. Aggressively recenter people of the global majority
13. Listen and respond with questions
14. Speak up (not over)
15. Accept accountability
16. Uncomfortably redistribute resources

Lastly, at the top of the pyramid is the co-conspirator tier. When in this tier, co-conspirators:

1. Listen to self-reflect
2. Stay vigilant
3. Act accountably
4. Take risks
5. Imagine and co-create
6. Pass the mic and the offering plate
7. Understand it's a lifestyle—they've learned how to go through the tough days and stay engaged

Intersectional Inquiry

- When you looked at the pyramid, where did you look first and why?
- What feelings arose for you?
- Many white folks have expressed concerns about the terms *co-conspirator* and *accomplice*. What would you say to them?
- Can you identify a time you were an active ally? What about an accomplice or co-conspirator? How did you know? And, most important, would a person of the targeted group agree with your assessment?

Practices

Now that we've explored some definitions and reoriented our starting point, we'll offer a few activities to help you, your children, and your parenting partners better explore your personal and social identities and build affirming language.

Before we dive in, we'd like to share a letter from Dr. Nicole Evans. Dr. Evans is a lifelong antiracist educator and community organizer who'd like to share her wisdom as she passes the torch to the next generation of antiracists.

Get into Good Trouble: A Letter from an Antiracist Elder

Your ancestors and elders want you to get into some good trouble, to spread seeds of freedom from your plentiful harvest so that your children and grandchildren and great-grandchildren can thrive!

With this work, I give you a seed to plant in the ground: a seed of freedom and joy for our Black, brown, and Indigenous children of color to feast from at the table of liberation! The ground has been watered with the tears of our ancestors, with sweat from our enslaved siblings working the fields on plantations, with blood from those such as Emmett Till, Tamir Rice, Breonna Taylor, George Floyd, and countless others brutally murdered for nothing more than having dark skin. The ground is ready to be tilled with the lessons that this book provides; the crops of liberty will be plentiful for the harvest!

With your work, this is possible.

—Dr. Nicole Evans

Rumination Practice

For parents and caregivers

Find a quiet place to think and write, and answer the questions below. If you need more writing space, grab a notebook and let each question inspire you to write as much as you'd like.

1. How do you define yourself? _____
   _____

2. What labels or identities do you immediately identify with? _____
   _____

3. What words have you used in the past that you now realize are inaccurate or harmful? _____
   _____

4. In what ways are you developing social justice language? _____
   _____

5. How can you help create safe, empathetic spaces? _____
   _____

6. How can you and your family help build community? _____
   _____

7. What are your family values, and how did your family decide on them? _____
   _____

Once done, sit with these answers and see if you've learned anything new about yourself through the answering process. If you have a parenting partner, consult each other after answering these questions to see the ways in which you have similar thinking and ways in which you have different thinking.

Who Am I?

For parents and caregivers

We all have personal and social identities. Your personal identity is what makes you unique. Your social identity is what you have in common with other people, like language(s), racialized identity, gender, sex, sexuality, worldview, socioeconomic status, abilities, and/or disabilities. Having social identities can create a sense of pride, connection, and community. In a white-dominated society, a nondominant identity can be minoritized or marginalized. Let's build language for how we see ourselves, and find the parts of ourselves that need affirming and the parts of ourselves that we can use in service of justice work.

Personal Identity

People can call me: _____

I'm most affirmed when people use _____ and _____ pronouns.

The places I call home are: _____

I live in a: _____

I like to spend my time: _____

I have learned to: _____

I am naturally talented at: _____

I celebrate my birth by: _____

My loved ones are: _____

I am always worried about: _____

I have been around the sun _____ times

Conflict causes me to: _____

When people look into my eyes, they will see: _____

I love spending time with: _____

What brings me hope is: _____

I believe in: _____

My favorite family meal is: _____

Great work tackling those questions. Now, say this affirmation out loud: *I'm an indispensable part of my community. I am valued, loved, and needed. I'm an antiracist committed to love, liberation, and justice.*

So, what did you already know about yourself going into this writing exercise? Was there anything new that helped you learn about yourself? Some things you can think about next are:

- Explore how you feel about who you are and who you are not.
- Ask yourself how you can use your unique characteristics to do racial justice work.
- Identify what areas you'll have to develop further to do racial justice work.
- List three ways you can continue to develop a confident personal identity.
- How can you begin to incorporate these questions and wonderings with the children in your life?

Who Am I? Part 2: Social Identity

For parents and caregivers

Now let's become comfortable with our social identities. Your responses are based on where you currently live, your social connections, and your current access to resources. When we're honest about our social identities, we're able to accurately identify where we hold immunities and where we're minoritized. This is extremely important (and quite exciting, if you ask me). It's how we know where to do the work and how to do the work.

Let's start to build language around these twelve social identities. These are certainly not all of the social identities; it's just a starting point.

1. The country I currently live in is: _____
2. My racialized identity is: _____
3. My ethnicity is: _____
4. My worldview is: _____
5. My gender is: _____
6. My physical ability is: _____
7. My family's socioeconomic status is: _____
8. My sexuality is: _____
9. My citizenship status is: _____
10. My sex is: _____
11. My home language is: _____
12. My mental health is: _____

Reflection:

- Which identities did you have language for right away?
- Which identities do you think about on a daily basis? For instance: when getting dressed, running errands, interviewing for a job, or taking care of your body?

- For which identities did you have to search for accurate language?
- Which identities do you feel comfortable, confident, or have a sense of pride in? Which identities do you notice you're hiding from coworkers, neighbors, or strangers?
- Which identities would you like to know more about?
- How can you begin to incorporate these questions and wonderings with the children in your life?

Check Your Privilege

For parents and caregivers

You may have heard the phrase "check your privilege," but many folks don't actually know where to start, or even how to identify when privilege is showing up in themselves. Try noticing when you are:

- Expecting or feeling entitled to time, energy, consideration, accommodation, smiles, or approval
- Receiving unearned resources (funds, materials, and employment opportunities)
- Receiving access to necessary resources that others don't have (food, transportation, water, health care, and education)
- Able to avoid conversations because they make you uncomfortable
- Able to be unaware, uninformed, uneducated, apolitical, or uncaring about others

Do this exercise regularly in order to build awareness and strengthen your ability to correct yourself, hold yourself accountable, and reorient yourself and your frame of mind.

We can't teach what we don't know, and we can't work with our children if we aren't committed to doing the work for ourselves first and foremost. If we're only willing to work with our children, but not yet ready to work on ourselves with our parenting partners and with family members, we'll simultaneously create opportunities for change and continued oppression. We must be willing to work with our peers, to create space for the truth and accountability. Otherwise, white children learn to be performative and children of the global majority are further harmed by the performance.

As you move forward in this book and in this antiracist practice, it's important to fully assess your starting place. Now that we've covered some basic definitions and discerned our points of reference, we can dive in. If you ever have difficulty remembering what certain terms mean, I encourage you to revisit this section so you can feel informed and secure in your understanding.

Finally, here are some key points to think about as you embark on this caregiving journey. We'll go more in-depth into these points throughout the book, but always try to keep them in mind as you're learning:

1. We live in a society with race-based outcomes, and that's not acceptable.
2. Race is a key determining factor in your success.
3. There's a system backing the deeply ingrained belief that white people are superior and entitled to dominate, creating white domination (supremacy).
4. Racism hasn't ended, it's evolved over time.
5. Approach racism with "systems-thinking."

healthy bodies

Part Two explores bodies, especially relating to children's understanding of race, health, body-positivity, feminism, and self-love. Through information and exercises for you and your child, we hope to guide you and your children to have a deeper, more loving understanding of their body and the bodies of those around them. This is imperative to do not only as parents and caregivers but as antiracist co-conspirators as well. As always, let's get grounded and know some resistance might be coming with the next few sections. Rise to the challenge to keep unlearning and relearning.

Children Are Constantly Absorbing Information

When I say children are never too young, I mean it. Young children are in a stage of dramatic growth and processing a lot of information. Infants through three-year-olds are actively learning on a subconscious level. Even though they're not working directly with you to construct their learning, learning is still happening through their exploration. Children three to five years old are collaborative beings, often asking, "What is it?" Through their questioning, they're inviting you into their world, sometimes as an expert, but most of the time as a partner. Children six to twelve years old enter into a period of intellectual growth, wondering, "Why is it?" This is where deeper, more explicit conversations about race might occur.

Lastly, don't be fooled by adolescent children's physical appearance and changes with puberty. They're still searching for themselves and peer acceptance. They're asking themselves, "How can I fit in?" and "How can I be myself?" Using these developmental themes, we can create practices to support our children's growth and awareness. As always, the exact timing of each stage will depend on the child. You know your child best. Use the ages listed as suggestions, not as hard-and-fast rules. Below are examples of antiracism awareness for the different age ranges to inform us of how we might approach discussions with them properly.

Twos	Threes and Fours	Fives
Notice differences in skin color	Continued curiosity about racial differences	Can begin to understand scientific explanations for differences in skin color, hair texture, and eye shape
Curious about differences in hair texture	Aware of prejudice toward skin color and other racial characteristics; becoming aware of societal bias against darker skin and other physical differences	Can understand more fully the range of racial differences and similarities
Use nonverbal cues to signal noticing differences; may react with curiosity or fear	Want to know how they got their hair color, skin color, and other characteristics	By five, Black and Latino children in research settings show no preference (prejudice) toward their own groups compared to white children; white children at this age remain strongly biased in favor of whiteness.

Twos	Threes and Fours	Fives
Overgeneralize common characteristics such as a skin color	Aware that getting older brings changes; may wonder if their skin, hair, and eye color remain constant	By kindergarten, children show many of the same racial attitudes that adults in our culture hold—they have already learned to associate some groups with higher status than others.
Children as young as two years use race to reason about people's behaviors.	Expressions of racial prejudice often peak at ages four and five.	Explicit conversations with five- to seven-year-olds about interracial friendship can dramatically improve their racial attitudes in as little as a single week.
By thirty months, most children use race to choose playmates.	Confusion about racial group names and actual color of their skin	

Elementary (typically ages five to twelve)	Adolescent (typically the teen years)
Can identify and critically think about interpersonal dynamics of racism, sexism, and classism, and other forms of -isms	"The search for personal identity intensifies in adolescents: vocational plans, religious beliefs, values and preferences, political affiliations and beliefs, gender roles, and ethnic identities" (Dr. Beverly Daniel Tatum).
Understand scientific explanations for phenotypes and adaptations	Aware of negative stereotypes and still may uphold these stereotypes
Understand the nature and harm of stereotyping and how to verbally interrupt them	Possible academic disinterest in school due to cultural and ethnic erasure in the curriculum

Elementary (typically ages five to twelve)	Adolescent (typically the teen years)
"After age 9, racial attitudes tend to stay constant unless the child experiences a life-changing event" (Frances Aboud, *Children & Prejudice* (New York: Basil Blackwell, 1988)).	Can be perceived as egocentric when really they assume their lived experiences are the same as their peers'
	When an individual identifies with a group as part of their social identity and that group is stereotyped in negative ways, the person is at risk of lower performance relative to the stereotyped dimension of that identity.

Featurism and Colorism

Over the centuries and into today, scientists, educators, clergy, and medical professionals have used pseudoscience to (1) categorize people into large invented racial groups, (2) successfully (unfortunately) assert racial groups to be predisposed to strengths, morality, and other race-based characteristics, and (3) accept racial disparities as normal.

We're still dealing with the impacts of American slavery and European colonization today. Featurism is an ugly and persistent impact affecting our children. **Featurism** is the practice of favoring Eurocentric skin color (colorism), hair texture (texturism), and certain physical features over non-Eurocentric features. Featurism is present in books, television shows, educational content, and even family conversations.

Colorism is a term coined by Alice Walker to describe the prejudicial or preferential treatment of people solely based on the color of their skin.[1] According to Margaret Hunter, "The maintenance of white supremacy (aesthetic, ideological, and material) is predicated on the notion that dark skin represents savagery, irrationality, ugliness, and inferiority. Whiteness itself is defined by the opposite: civility, rationality, beauty, and superiority. These contrasting definitions are the foundation for colorism."[2] It's important to know that adolescents are especially sensitive to the ways our society centers lighter skin and European features.

When Carter was thirteen years old, he asked me if Hispanic people can be Black. When explaining to him that Hispanic and/or Latine/x people represent a wide variety of racial identities and skin colors, because race is not the same as ethnicity, it was important to be curious about where the confusion was stemming from. We learned through our discussion that colorism in TV, movies, music, and the media had limited his experience with the vastly diverse cultures, racialized identities, and history of the Latinidad community. He had only ever seen light-skinned Latine/x/Hispanic individuals in movies and on television. This lack of exposure to any Afro-Latine/x or Indigenous Latine/x representation caused confusion. It's important to think about this issue, colorism, and their connection when consuming media, building connections, and navigating your and your child's identity.

This is not a coincidence. Colorism is a seed planted by white domination. Which version of communities of color are "most acceptable"? Which can align themselves most closely with whiteness, privilege, and Eurocentric beauty standards? Usually, it's the light-skinned version of Blackness or brownness that's featured and appreciated, both from within and from outside their respective communities.

Colorism outcomes can be noted in all four domains:

Internalized: Dark-skinned adolescents more likely to have lower body image and lower self-esteem.

Interpersonal: Name-calling.

Institutional: Girls with very dark skin tones are three times more likely to be suspended from school than girls with very light skin tones.

Systemic: Very light skin increases likelihood of attending college and being employed full-time.

Colorism isn't only about skin color. Historically and contemporarily, Black hair is discriminated against consistently. Black people have experienced anti–curly hair discrimination from the beginning of enslavement. This preference for straight hair over curly hair (texturism) has led to hair-based discrimination both in school and in the workforce.[3] Straight hair is often seen as more professional (read: white), while curly hair is seen as unprofessional. Hair-based discrimination has led to the natural hair movement and now the CROWN Act. To be clear, as antiracist folks, we believe Black women, gender-nonconforming people, nonbinary people, and queer folks should have every right to wear their hair in a style that honors their culture, protects their hair from damage, and makes them feel empowered.

Using our antiracist skills, we can use this information to drive our responses to our children's questions and work to end discrimination. This background information, along with children's developmental themes, helps us respond to their budding curiosity. We know that children as young as two years old are curious about where they "got" certain characteristics. We can start to use simple scientific explanations, using the language below, when responding to their "Why is it?" questions.

> "You have darker skin because your dad and I passed along our
>   skin color to you."
> "You have more almond-shaped eyes because your mama
>   shared her eye shape with you."
> "Your genetic instructions from your dad and me dictated the
>   color of your hair."

If their questions are about physical differences in other people, we can use the same foundation: "Well, they received their _____ from their parents." I also like to add, "We're different, and we all get to be different." Embracing your children's curiosity will support them in becoming open-minded, science-driven, and empathetic. Differences do not divide us; it's our fear and unfair treatment of differences that do. It's always important to stress that there's not a superior characteristic, and it's never okay to treat others unfairly because of their differences.

For white families, conditionally white families, and light-skinned families working to combat colorism and featurism, the first step is to notice how whiteness is being centered in your home. Take a look at the magazines you purchase, and the books, TV shows, and movies your children consume. Notice how many of the characters and people have straight hair or are white-passing or light-skinned. Seek out images and materials featuring dark-skinned people and very curly hair. In my own home, I make it a practice to print out pictures and paste them on top of the white children in my children's homeschooling worksheets.

At school, start with your child's teachers. Reach out if you notice colorism and featurism in the classroom and have an open discussion with the teachers to rectify the issue and include representation of different features and races. You can also partner with other parents to address this if you don't feel comfortable doing it alone, or if you're met with some hesitation or resistance on the teacher's part.

Why Do We Look Different?

Race as a biological category isn't real (really, it's true!), but racism as a social issue and construct *is*. Racial groups aren't all that genetically distinct or scientifically significant in their differences. In the following sections, we break down the ways white domination, history, and current cultural and societal standards shape our relationships to our bodies, and how we can work to counteract negative influences so our children can have healthier bodily relationships. The next few sections are written in a conversational tone. Feel empowered to borrow any of my language that feels right for you to use with your children when having conversations.

Starting with Young Children

The United States has a long, ugly, and complicated history when it comes to race and racism. But our story shouldn't start with racism—it should begin with skin tones, phenotypes, and history.

Young children are very concrete thinkers, so it's best not to use idioms, metaphors, or socially and politically created terms to explain big concepts. If you ask a child to "show me the black crayon," they'll pick the crayon we've all agreed is black. If you ask a young child to "show me a Black person," they'll look for a person who matches the color of the crayon.

We begin our work with simple biology lessons. Skipping over these scientific lessons does not tend to young children's need to understand the world around them—or to understand themselves. A solid lesson should both affirm a child's skin tone and offer a scientific explanation.

Here's a little background information for the parenting partners: As early humans migrated around the world, our ancestors adapted to the different environments. It's a biological process that randomly takes place, and the changes happen over time. There are lots of examples of plants and animals adapting over time. Modern humans aren't any different; over time, adaptation has created a diversity of phenotypes. Phenotypes are our physical characteristics, both visible like hair and eye color and measurable like height and weight, plus our personality, behavior, and other parts of our development. Some phenotypes are developed because of epigenetics, while others are environmental and lifestyle factors.

Now start chatting about human differences with your young child. Remember to approach conversations with curiosity:

- I have skin. You have skin. We all have skin. But I wonder why we have skin. What does our skin do for us?
- Can you name everyone's largest organ? "Body organs aren't all internal like the brain or the heart. There's one we wear on the outside. Skin is our largest organ—adults carry around eight pounds of it. This fleshy covering does a lot more than make us look presentable. In fact, without it, we'd literally evaporate!"[4]
- Have you ever thought about what's so incredible about skin? Our skin is one of our biggest protectors. It keeps our insides dry. It helps keep us cool or warm. And it helps protect our body from damaging sunlight.
- Have you ever wondered why some people have different skin tones? Everyone gets their skin color from something called melanin. The amount of melanin we have is determined by an invisible genetic code that our parents give us. Some people have more melanin than others. The more melanin the darker the skin color, so the less melanin the lighter or paler the skin. What other questions do you have?

Phenotype Introduction

For children ages three to nine years old

When introducing the concept of phenotypes to your child, pair the discussion with a research activity the two of you can do together.

1. Research migration routes.
2. Read a children's book (or articles) about contemporary immigration.
3. Complete the phenotype chart below.

Examples of Phenotype	
My skin color is . . .	My hair texture is . . .
My hair color is . . .	My hairline is . . .
I can('t) digest milk without symptoms.	I can('t) roll my tongue.
I have/don't have freckles.	I can('t) extend my thumb.
My eye color is . . .	I can('t) clasp my hands.
My shoe size is . . .	My earlobes are(n't) attached.
My height is . . .	I have/don't have dimples.

Introducing Race, Racialized Identities, and Racism

Race scientists are scientists who believe race is biological or genetic. Race scientists invented five large categories to lump groups of people based on physical characteristics, geographical location, and cultural ties. But they didn't stop there; race scientists then went on to place these invented racial groups in an order of superior to inferior. This science is wrong, and I refer to it as pseudoscience. Race is actually a social (community) and political (laws and policies) creation. Our government, the military, the education system, the health-care system, the banking system, and everyday people have used this pseudoscience to continue race-based discrimination and classification. True science has shown that race as a biological category isn't real.

This misuse of power, science, and money is racism, a system of advantage based on racial discrimination. White people are advantaged, receiving privileges and immunities, while people of the global majority are disadvantaged. Race science is still used today, and we must notice and confront when people are using it to justify and accept racial discrimination.

If race isn't real, then why do we discuss it? Can we just ignore it and it will all go away?

Unfortunately, no. Our societies have been structured to be unequal. Racism acts like an invisible machine, operating to support, uplift, and help white people automatically. At this point, we need to build an antiracist machine. Our antiracist machine will notice who's operating the machine, who is unfairly benefiting from its work, and who needs to be centered to counteract it. We'll also notice through our own antiracist mechanism who's experiencing injustice and discrimination, and how we can use our agency to support antiracism to combat them.

Race has a lot to do with the way people will interact with you, for better or worse. It doesn't have anything to do with your personality, abilities, or knowledge. We live in a racist society, and that means every single person has a racialized identity. By seven years old, white children can use racialized language to self-identify. It's important for white children to recognize themselves as having a racialized body and to develop an identity based on reality and not supremacy or toxicity.

Being Body-Positive—for Yourself and for Your Kids

Acknowledging the beauty and power of bodies typically overlooked by society goes beyond just conversations about race. Society's ideas of worth and acceptability not only focus on whiteness, but also on thinness, bodies without disabilities, heterosexuality, and masculinity more often than not. In order to properly model that your child should love, respect, and value all bodies, we must also model those ideals in ourselves. How we love and respect our own bodies can influence and affect how we love and respect others'.

Society helps us build and strengthen the muscles for self-criticism and self-hate from an early age. Rarely do we have the muscles to exercise self-love on the regular. Our children are always learning and watching, receiving messages about what is good, beautiful, or correct. These messages can have lasting impacts. Self-love is not just for you: it's for everyone watching you and learning from you.

Loving the Bigger Body

I grew up in a fat-phobic household. I watched my mother relentlessly dieting, being self-conscious on every family vacation, purchasing clothes to try on at home instead of in the fitting room, using me as a prop in pictures to shield her body from view, and enjoying her restaurant desserts in the car instead of at the table with us. I never saw my mother love her body, enjoy her body, or be grateful for all of the amazing things her body could do. I grew up fearing becoming fat, not because of the health implications, but because of the way society bullies, stereotypes, and discriminates against fat people.

Sabrina Strings documents how fat phobia is rooted in racism in her 2019 book *Fearing the Black Body*. She documents how pseudoscience was used to prove European-white women were naturally disciplined, superior, and rational thinkers, resulting in thinner bodies. Simultaneously, this depicted enslaved Black women as lazy, overly sexual beings who were gluttonous. Race scientists worked to prove Black bodies were fat, indulgent, and had venereal diseases to justify the control of women and the enslavement of Black women. This race science also contributed to Black women's dehumanization and further divided white women, free Black women, and enslaved Black women. Most important, it's led to the continued discrimination, alienation, and denigration of fat women, women of color, and fat people in general.

Since I grew up in a fat-phobic household, I know it's my responsibility to interrupt the cycle of body-shaming. When I hear loved ones making remarks about a person's body, I immediately interrupt with, "Bodies are just bodies. All bodies are worthy bodies. It's *not* okay to comment on someone's body." When my children were in the stage where they were commenting on my body, I made it a point to say "I love my body, it belongs to me" or "That's not your concern." A fantastic figure in the radical self-love space, especially regarding body positivity, is Sonya Renee Taylor. Her book *The Body Is Not an Apology* is a must-read for any and all folks interested in undoing the work of oppression regarding their own bodies.

What Messages Are You Sending Your Child?

As I'm raising two cisgender boys (self-identified), I want my children to know that being healthy and being skinny are not the same thing. While we live in a society that's obsessed with eating "healthy foods," "the right foods," and "good foods," we're sending our children the message that (1) food contains morality, (2) healthy only equates to the food we eat, and (3) healthiness is determined by individuals making "good" choices. In this section, we'll talk about food culture and all of its complexities, and the way we can support our children's relationship with food.

Respecting Food Culture

Using our antiracist lens, we can unpack the inequality of food: how certain foods are inaccessible to certain populations and communities, and how certain food holds negative connotations, or are appropriated and colonized. We can also analyze what other factors are left out of the health conversation that are impacting the quality of life for Black and brown folks. Lastly, we should remember that food is a community-building thing.

Children are living in a time when the "perfect body" is praised by media, their peers, and even their family. Social media in particular has exacerbated this issue. It's important to explore the activities provided at the end of this section to build a strong positive self-identity and concept. As parenting partners, we can educate ourselves about eating disorders—which affect children regardless of gender and race—and continue the necessary work of self-acceptance.

We should aim for our children to understand:

1. How they can care for and appreciate themselves
2. Body size does not represent health status

Respecting the Disabled Body

Before engaging in antiracist work, I never considered how social structures created access. I just went about my everyday life, accessing the world through my own abilities. If I was shopping and my cart couldn't fit through the narrow aisle, I simply left my cart, picked up what I needed, and came back. It didn't occur to me that the aisle was designed for my body's specific abilities. What about a person who uses a wheelchair or walker or has a sighted guide? Now that I have this awareness, I'm able to flag down a manager to notify them that the aisle is not accessible for everyone and wait while team members rearrange the rolling carts.

When we're walking and the sidewalk is broken, I stop to say to my children, "Look at this sidewalk. Who does this hurt? Is this unfair to anyone?" At this point, my children can answer, "People who use wheelchairs, people with strollers or carts, or someone who's unstable with walking." Then we jump into action together: we call 311 to report it. It's not that it's just an inconvenience, it's inaccessibility that needs to be resolved.

To build the muscles of curiosity and awareness with my children, we're still doing our never-ending identity work. *Who am I? Who am I not? Where do I hold immunities, privilege, and marginalization?* Then we analyze, together, how we're able to access resources, places, institutions, and media to learn about and address these inequities. Our family uses social media to listen to and learn from the disabled community, to learn about accurate language and ways we can use our agency to make change. I encourage you and your family to follow disabled activists and advocates to hear about their experiences and support their success.

I want my children to understand disability is both visible and invisible, that it happens on a spectrum and can change. Disability could refer to a person's physical, mental, intellectual, or emotional state. People with disabilities can experience discrimination based on inaccessibility (lack of elevators, lack of accessible parking spots, or broken infrastructure) and also verbal harassment ("crazy," "stupid," "dumb," "slow"). As we learn, we can hold each person accountable. I might use the term *crazy*, a term we know now is rooted in ableism, and my children give me the gift of truth: "Mom, remember, it's 'wild' or 'bananas.'"

For my family, the one we had to unpack and name the most was the inspiration porn that fills our social media feeds. *Inspiration porn* was a term coined by the disability rights activist Stella Young as a genre of media depictions of disabled people. It assumes that disability is always a tragedy and that people with disabilities should be pitied and infantilized, there's an uplifting moral message aimed at non-disabled viewers, and disabled people are reduced to objects in the message. Watching Young's 2014 TED Talk with the family is a good start to learn more about this.

Checklist for Identifying Inspiration Porn

Spotting inspiration porn can be tricky. Here are four questions our family uses to help us analyze media:

- Why is this inspiring?
- Was it created for likes and shares?
- Is it using a disabled person or person with a disability as motivation for non-disabled people?
- Was it created by the person being praised or another person?

Patriarchy, Racism, and Feminism: Your Children and Their Self-Expression

Our relationship with our body is heavily influenced by the images presented to us, how people we love treat us, and how strangers react to us. Open a magazine, scroll through social media, or roam the mall and we can begin to notice beauty trends. **Beauty trends** are mainstream examples of what are acceptable and preferred. All of these trends are influenced by racism and sexism and, in turn, influence how our children express themselves. As a child, I learned our bodies did not belong to us; they belonged to strangers, our life partners, our places of employment, and the male gaze.

Understanding the history and the context about how bodies have been regulated by laws and institutions, treated as property, vilified in the media, and regularly debated allows us to analyze and appreciate layers of body oppression. Children need multiple perspectives to actively explore these layers of oppression and to find patterns of discrimination. We can practice feminism and learn to think critically about the patriarchy to provide a richer context around gender, women's history, and the vast complexities of the women's movement and body autonomy.

The **patriarchy**, like white domination, is an ideological oppression that places cisgender men on top of the social, political, and economic hierarchy. The patriarchy also works hand in hand with white domination to place fairer-skinned (white) women above dark-skinned women. This means all women experience gender-based discrimination, but the intensity and the types of discrimination are going to feel and look different. Like white domination, there are undercurrents of morality and what it means (and looks like) to be a "good" girl, woman, or wife within the patriarchy.

The patriarchy harms men as well. When Carter was three, he loved playing with my old cell phone that happened to have a hot-pink case. At the time, my partner was completely opposed to it, concerned that playing with pink would "send the wrong message." This small moment of fear was a learning opportunity for both of us. My partner had deep misunderstandings about gender, sexuality, and how they're formed and developed. While he was unlearning, Carter was learning that colors are for everyone. There's no such thing as a girl color or boy color. A decade later we can giggle about it, but back then it wasn't so funny. It's important for us to acknowledge how our misunderstandings will limit our children in becoming their fullest selves.

Men often experience low self-esteem because of societal expectations of desirable masculine traits they might not have. Within the patriarchy, homophobia, misogyny, and sexism are intertwined. Boys and men are expected to subscribe to certain ideals of masculinity and interpersonal dynamics (physical, emotional, and mental) that discourage them from being vulnerable, emotional, or gentle, which can be associated as feminine attributes. Our boys resist straying from a predisposed ideal of manliness, typically to preserve the immunities that come from the patriarchy, and to avoid ever being conceived as "gay" or "effeminate." This fear leads to troubled relationships with themselves and with others, especially women. If our boys aren't exploring gender and gender expression, they can't reach their fullest potential and can't fully feel comfortable accepting others. If our boys feel as though there's only one right way to look and act, they won't be able to handle a world that differs from that belief. It's important to raise our children with the space to be vulnerable, and with the understanding that masculinity is not superior, and that there's no one right way to exist.

Parenting and Gender Roles

"Dad, do you remember when you would take me to soccer practice after school, and when the practice was over, I'd always find you sleeping in the car?" As a parent, I admire how involved my dad was in our caretaking, even while working full-time. My mom was pursuing her PhD and teaching full-time for most of my childhood. I never once heard my parents discuss who would cook dinner, fold the laundry, or take me to practice or games. It was always my dad. My mom checked our homework, took us back-to-school shopping (thank the Lord!), and was our confidante. But Dad was our primary caretaker; it was an unspoken fact.

This isn't unusual in the Black community, either. I would be remiss if I didn't take a moment to debunk a commonly held stereotype about Black fathers. The idea of "absent" Black fathers is misrepresentative and damaging. A CDC study found that "Black fathers (70 percent) were most likely to have bathed, dressed, diapered, or helped their children use the toilet every day compared with white (60 percent) and Hispanic fathers (45 percent)." Black fathers are more actively involved in their children's lives than any of their counterparts. Just as Black women face stereotypes, Black men are portrayed as lazy, slow, and too cynical to attempt to change their position in life. These stereotypes were born out of American slavery—false ideals to justify the continued enslavement of Black people. Then, in 1965, a report called "The Negro Family: The Case for National Action" was published by a white sociologist and the then Assistant Secretary of Labor, Daniel Patrick Moynihan. He falsely asserted that "out-of-wedlock" births and single-mother homes were the destruction of the Black community.

So where does this myth come from? First, Moynihan and others have made the illogical assumption that being unmarried equals being absent; it doesn't. Using heteronormative, white-patriarchal marriage standards to judge Black families misses the trust, strength, and knowledge that is alive in the Black community. Many mothers self-report a very different story than the one imagined in Moynihan's report, sharing how they actively co-parent with their children's fathers, discussing parenting agreements, schedules, bedtimes, and more. Further, many share stories that include grandparents, godparents, aunts, and uncles in the childrearing process. This collective and communal upbringing needs to be represented in children's media, children's books, and parenting books. Second, the Black community faces a deep systemic attack that is taking Black fathers from their children. It's called racism. We'll dive deeper into our country's mass incarceration, police brutality, and unequal health outcomes later in the book. As a family, beware of the way families are portrayed and discussed in your household. Seek out non-heteronormative images and puzzles to represent family dynamics. Last, always insist that families are different. There's no right way or one way to be a family.

The Power of Playtime

I firmly believe that all children, regardless of age, need time to play. Playing happens across all cultures; it's a universal language of children. Play is intrinsically motivating—it involves the child's whole self (their body, their mind, their emotions); it requires a great deal of concentration—the child is in charge of constructing their imagination; and it requires curiosity and persistence. My favorite part of play is seeing how inclusive play can be with children. You might see one child using a stroller while another child wears a baby-carrier. One child might be preparing sushi rolls while another child fries catfish in their play kitchen. Let's use playful opportunities with our children to embrace language for differences. While playing we can model new language, and we can listen to hear how they're constructing their world and creating space for differences to be included.

Playtime is also an incredible opportunity to observe our children exploring gender roles. Because children are experiencing gender stereotypes from the very beginning (gender reveals, nursery colors, gendered clothing, gendered toys, and gendered language), they've already internalized what's right according to society. They're copying what they're witnessing and taking mental notes of who is doing what. To help our three-to-five-year-olds—regardless of their gender—to play the cook, the caretaker, the nurse, the dentist, the princess, the construction worker, etc., we start by modeling. In our house, my partner and I take turns planning and preparing dinner, making appointments, and doing drop-off and pickup at school. When I notice more of the caretaking and domestic duties are falling on my plate, I name it at dinnertime in front of the children, and my partner does the same. Our children are listening to us discuss gender roles, responsibilities, and partnership. For roles outside the house, we're intentional in who we choose to support and uplift as models of their profession. Dentists, pediatricians, fitness trainers, accountants, and other service providers whom you have the autonomy to choose are all professions to consider. When it's not possible, check out children's books that disrupt gender stereotypes.

During play, if a child says, "You can't be the doctor, you're a girl," or "You can't sew, you're a boy," we must be ready to identify these as gendered stereotypes and respond to help each child learn differently:

> "That's not accurate. There are women doctors. We just don't have one."
>
> "People know how to sew because they practice. Sewing is a skill that anyone can learn. Boys, girls, and nonbinary people can all learn to sew."

Gender, Sexuality, and Self-Expression

Everyone has a gender identity. People express themselves in many ways, such as through clothes, makeup, or hairstyles. Some people think certain expressions go with certain genders, but honestly, clothes, hairstyles, toys, occupations, and colors belong to everyone. We can't guess someone's gender or pronouns from how they look, which is why it's important to ask. Gender identity is all about how you feel—girl, boy, both, neither. We can ask children what pronouns they use and model using our pronouns whenever possible: "I'm most affirmed by she/her pronouns; how about you?" Or "If someone is retelling a story about you, what are all the names they can call you?" Since we don't want to misgender someone, we can use the universal "they" until we know a person's gender.

If someone roller-skates on the sidewalk, we can simply say, "I would like to roller-skate like them." If someone bagged our groceries, we can simply say, "I always appreciate how the bagger asks for my reusable bags." Actively and consistently modeling this level of awareness and caring regarding gender and respect is imperative for children to develop their own awareness and self-respect. This is important beyond basic ideas of respect; it also promotes safety and acceptance for transgender and gender-nonconforming individuals. Lastly, we're not always entitled to know someone's gender, either. Please know that not everyone is comfortable with sharing their gender or pronouns, because the space might not be welcoming. If you're cisgender, it's your responsibility to work to make the space welcoming.

Sexuality, Gender, and Racism

With young children, I introduce sexuality through adult relationships and family dynamics. I like to ask: "Who is in their family?" When discussing a same-sex family, it's important to note to children that no one is "missing." I reserve the word *missing* for family members who have died or are physically separated due to immigration, incarceration, or employment. The overall theme for young children is to understand that "Families are different."

School Dress Codes

While white supremacy and the patriarchy stereotype white girls as innocent, kind, and fragile, the stereotypes are different for Black girls, and this impacts school dress codes and discipline outcomes. Oftentimes, these dress codes focus on controlling girls' bodies as a way to "protect" them. School personnel have been known to line girls up at lunchtime and measure their tank top straps, sending those with straps too skinny home, to change, or to in-school suspension. Other girls reportedly have school personnel enter their classrooms to measure their short and skirt lengths. This message reinforces that girls need to cater to boys and their limits or preferences. It also sends the message that girls need to be overly concerned with what they wear, and that if something bad happens, they'll be blamed for their poor clothing choices. Black girls also face compounding discrimination. Let's look at twin sisters Mya and Deanna Cook, who attended Mystic Valley Regional Charter School with braided hair extensions in 2017. The sixteen-year-old Black girls received several infractions, were repeatedly asked to step out of class, and were given detention. This was also true for other Black girls with hair extensions. Parents of the twins pointed out to administrators that white girls wearing extensions, as pictured in the school's yearbook, were not punished. This is not an isolated event, either. Dorinda J. Carter Andrews, assistant dean of equity outreach initiatives at Michigan State University, says that "Black females are more likely to receive harsher discipline than their white and Latina counterparts." And it starts earlier than we think: new data shows that adults view Black girls as less innocent and more adultlike than their white peers, especially in the age range of five to fourteen.[5] Antiracist feminism instead would ask, what are the disparate outcomes girls are facing today? Who is causing the harm? How can we hold them accountable for their actions instead of victim-blaming?

While the goal of school dress codes is supposedly to attempt to minimize distraction in the classroom, these policies and their disciplinary consequences disrupt the learning environment for students, disproportionately students of color and girls.[6] As antiracist parents and caregivers, you can advocate for policy change in schools and critique those ones currently in place to make dress codes more equitable in the future. When reading student handbooks or hearing from your children about unfair or outdated enforced policies, look into getting your parenting partners together and scheduling a town hall or a meeting with teachers and school administrators to go over these policies. Focus on the harmful, disparate outcomes associated with them. This is exactly what students, parents, and families in Seattle did: "The Seattle School Board voted to adopt a districtwide student dress policy for the first time. With the creation of this policy, unnecessary subjective views of appropriate school attire have been eliminated, instead supporting school staff in focusing their time and efforts on educating students."[7] Their policy reads:

Students must wear:

- Top (shirt, blouse, sweater, sweatshirt, tank, etc.);
- Bottom (pants, shorts, skirt, dress, etc.); and
- Footwear

The emphasis of this policy is on equitable treatment of students and regulation of student dress must be free from bias. Students will no longer be disciplined or removed from class as a consequence for their attire, and staff will use reasonable efforts to avoid shaming students . . . Student attire enforcement will not create disparities in class time or increase marginalization of any group. No student shall be referred to as a "distraction" due to their attire.[8]

Exploring the Gender Spectrum with Your Children

For children of all ages, learning happens while playing and watching. This is a practice that you can try when reading books with children, watching television, watching movies, playing with toys, and/or at the grocery store.

Here's a small reading list of children's books that work to re-center Black, Brown, Indigenous, and Asian folks and affirm the gender spectrum:

- *Pink Is Just a Color and So Is Blue*, by Niki Bhatia
- *We Are Water Protectors*, by Carole Lindstrom
- *Mama Says Homebirth*, by Miquilaue Young
- *Fuego, Fuegito / Fire, Little Fire*, by Jorge Argueta
- *Say Something!* by Peter H. Reynolds
- *Eyes That Kiss in the Corners*, by Joanna Ho
- *Mela and the Elephant*, by Dow Phumiruk
- *Little Night*, by Yuyi Morales
- *Like the Moon Loves the Sky*, by Hena Khan

Many cultures around the world acknowledge and validate trans and gender-fluid experiences that live across a spectrum. Here are a few examples:

- *Hijra*: South Asia
- *Yan daudu*: Northern Nigeria
- *Muxe*: Zapotec cultures of Oaxaca, Mexico
- *Fa'afine*: Samoa
- *Fakaleiti*: Tonga
- *Mahu*: Hawai'i
- *Burrnesha*: Albania
- *Kathoey*: Thailand (while this term can refer to feminine transgender identities, the term is sometimes used pejoratively)[9]

Many times, families who actively work toward disrupting white domination culture are learning alongside their children. As adults, we may unintentionally reinforce gender binaries and norms that confuse or cause harm. Acknowledging when we're doing this out loud can demonstrate to children that making mistakes is an important part of the process that'll take us to a more liberated, aware community.

Take some time to reflect on how you're implementing this practice in your day-to-day routine with your children. Ask yourself questions such as:

- Did you choose your gender identity? Was it imposed on you?
- How does this practice affirm your own gender identity exploration?
- What statements would you add to this list?
- What questions would you add to this list?
- What further learning do you have in regards to the gender spectrum?

—Maribel Gonzalez

Practices

Building Agency Through Affirmations and Activities: A Home Filled with Love and Respect

In the following section, there will be many affirming activities for you and your children to try. Many of these activities are affirming for families of the global majority. For white families, many of these activities can have variations to help confront bias and educate. There are a variety of activities that will help you to establish concepts of self-love, respect, and identity affirmation through practices in your home. Find the practices that resonate with you first, then work up to finding (and creating) practices that challenge you. Each practice can be revisited; as your child is in a different stage of development, return to the practice to revisit it from a different angle.

Prompts for Parenting Partners

The questions below are inspired by the book *Anti-Bias Education for Young Children and Ourselves* by Louise Derman Sparks and Julie Olsen Edwards. I encourage you to read the book when you have the chance.

1. When did you begin to notice human differences: skin tones, eye shapes, hair texture, and hair color? Were you ever encouraged to think about racial differences by the adults around you?
2. Identify a few messages you received from your family, school, faith-based community, and media about racial diversity, body sizes, health, gender, and sexuality. Were you ever actively encouraged to be inclusive and accepting?
3. How do you feel today discussing human differences, race, diversity, and racism? Do you feel you have the tools to have conversations with the adults in your life? Do you feel comfortable discussing this with your children?

Building an Inclusive Future

For families with children ages six to ten years old

Here's an example of how you can encourage recentering and consideration when playing:

> *Child:* "Mom, will you build something with me?"
> *Adult:* "Yes! I'm imagining building a school. Would you like to build that with me?"
> *Child:* "Let's do it!"

Start building right away, and notice who your child is building for. When they're building for themselves, encourage them to think about their neighbors. Building structures is the perfect time to practice accessibility. As you build, naturally ask: "Where do we want to build our school? What do you want in our school?"

As you're building, here are a few possible phrases:

1. Let's have plenty of water bottle stations inside and out.
2. How about a gymnasium, with a swimming pool attached. Should we add a lift into the pool?
3. We can't forget about bathrooms. Let's put in four gender-neutral bathrooms with TVs and sofas!
4. What about a rooftop garden, with an elevator?
5. Where would the babies sleep and play? Where would the teenagers hang out? Should we create an elder rec room? What do they need to be welcomed here?
6. Let's build an accessible playground here, like the one by our house.

One of the things I love about antiracism is the playful imagination we practice. Playful imagination allows us to envision an entirely new world. We're playing with the idea of building something for everyone. Antiracist children think about their neighbors, and create structures and places centered around inclusivity. Just think about it: We wouldn't have to ask people to "fit in" if the place was created for them by design.

Encourage children to understand that their imagination can be used to reenvision their current world; they can completely redesign things to be more equitable, magical, and creative. Antiracist children can imagine about their neighbors, create new wondrous structures, and design places centered around inclusivity.

Affirming Activity: Taking Up Space

A Lifestyle Practice for Black and Brown Caregivers

Much of my parenting has mimicked policing, controlling my children's bodies, voices, and presence. My children anticipate being limited in public spaces. I noticed myself restricting movement in public, hushing my children for just simply being who they are: kids. As a Black woman, I know what it's like to be surveilled, watched, and controlled. Instead of offering my children choice, freedom, and trust, I projected my internalized (appropriated) racial oppression onto them hoping to protect them from situations like this.

Once I was grocery shopping with my preschool- and toddler-aged children. While I was looking at the store items, my children were moving and wiggling about the space (as young kids tend to do). Suddenly, a white man came up to them and yelled: "Stop doing that!" I was stunned and traumatized. I was a new parent and completely unprepared for this situation. I want Black and brown children to receive the same compassion or allowances that white children do. I was unprepared for the level of aggression directed at my children by a total stranger for existing in a way many kids do: freely and energetically.

If that situation were to happen again, I would stand up for my children. I would tell that man that he had no right to talk to my children like that and to mind his business. To all my Black and brown caregivers, TAKE UP AS MUCH SPACE as you want and let it be a lifestyle practice.

In order for us to practice freedom with children, we have to get comfortable with our own practice. I offer you this simple meditation for these moments. Say this with your children or by yourself whenever you feel like you need to.

This is your reminder to take a deep breath
Let the breath take up space in your lungs
Let it fill you with freedom and joy

Let it be the reminder that you deserve
To feel at home in your body
And you have the right to practice your freedom
in a world that is not yet healed

The beauty of a constant ritual
That holds us in our humanity

Continue to practice your inner liberation and get free
Continue to honor your ancestors with every breath and allow
yourself to sink into joy
like fully lounge in those moments of absolute delight
let your children witness your freedom
And in doing so, they follow

—Amelia Allen Sherwood

Affirming Music Activities: Make a Playlist!

For families with children of all ages

Music is powerful! Music affects our mood and our attitude. Work with your children to build affirmative playlists that make them want to move freely. Find a theme song for self-affirmation and empowerment.

Here are the top ten songs from my household as an example:

1. "To Be Young, Gifted and Black" by Nina Simone
2. "Luna Lovers" by Las Cafeteras
3. "Don't Worry Be Happy" by Bobby McFerrin
4. "Tuwe Tuwe" by Sweet Honey In The Rock
5. "Change the World" by Alphabet Rockers
6. "Jump Jump" by Kris Kross
7. "One Love/People Get Ready" by Bob Marley
8. "All I Really Need" by Raffi
9. "I Got You" by James Brown
10. "When We Grow Up" by Diana Ross

Conversations about Racial Identities

For parents and caregivers

The steps in this activity can be done by parents and caregivers to better inform and prepare conversations about racial identities with the children in their lives. If you're unsure how to describe or best respect and acknowledge a certain person's racial identity to your child, our suggestion is to research the individual to see how they identify themselves. If you like, you can also perform this research with your children.

1. Read biographies: Research the person to know exactly how they identify and use the language the person uses when discussing them with your children. You're indirectly teaching: (1) each person chooses the language that feels affirming to them, and (2) we honor and acknowledge how people identify. When introducing the person, share a bit about their personal story and include their social indicators.

   Example: Showing a picture of Dr. King, then saying, "Do you know who this person is? This is Dr. Martin Luther King, Jr. We'll call him Dr. King. Dr. King helped organize millions of people to combat racism. Dr. King was a husband, father, and friend. He identified as a Christian Black man. Let's watch this clip of him together." (Then, play *Dr. King: I'm Black and I'm Proud!*)

2. When I'm filling out forms, my children are right there with me. I verbally say my name, phone number, and address. I also verbally identify my social indicators:

   * "I identify as Black American."
   * "I identify as a female."
   * "Oh, they didn't include my ethnicity. I'll have to choose non-Hispanic."

3. If and when it comes up organically, we ask our family members how they identify themselves.

Note: All people in the United States have racialized bodies. It's crucial that white adults identify as being white, naming whiteness and discussing their racialized identities. This helps young children be realistic about their whiteness and not expect it to be the default. Oftentimes, families of the global majority will use a mixture of both racialized identities and ethnicities to identify themselves, and this fluidity is welcomed.

Arts and Crafts: Affirming Features

For families with children ages two to eight years old

Self-portraits are a wonderful way to support your child in developing self-love and self-understanding. Stock your home with these arts-and-crafts goodies to help them explore.

Encourage your children to use the materials below when creating and drawing, but also allow for creativity. Don't be alarmed if your child of the global majority chooses to paint themselves green or another color; it might just be their favorite color. By providing these materials in your home, you're normalizing different skin colors and providing the opportunity for them to accurately portray themselves.

What you'll need:

- Skin-tone crayons
- Skin-tone markers
- Skin-tone paint
- Skin-tone colored pencils
- Skin-tone construction paper
- Sticker eyes (look to represent real eye colors and shapes)
- Yarn to represent hair color
- A hand-held mirror

Using the handheld mirror, ask your child to focus on one part of their face (eyes, lips, mouth, nose, ears, etc.). Practice drawing and coloring each part. While working, have a conversation about this body part, focusing on affirmation.

- "My lips are for kissing you good night. What are your lips for?"
- "What are three things you love about your face?"
- "What is the color of your _____?"

Arts and Crafts: Making Skin-Tone Paint

For families with Black and brown children of all ages. Variations are detailed
for families with white children.

One of my favorite activities to do with my children is mixing colors to make *their* skin tone. You can use this skin-tone paint to make portraits, self-portraits, or to paint with in general. This activity can be repeated several times over the coming years. When children are older, they can work to create different skin tones, blush tones, hair color, eye color, and more.

1. Mix together equal parts of red, blue, and yellow. Less is best in the beginning. This will create a beautiful deep brown.
2. Now allow your child to add a little black (only a little) or white depending on their particular shade.
3. Allow the child to paint the skin tone on their arm to see if it matches. "Does this match your skin?" We aren't looking for perfection, we're looking for the child to love and find beauty in their skin tone.
4. Once the child finds their match, we can make more paint to save for later projects. Bottle the extra in a one-ounce container. Ask the child, "What color would you call this?" Then label the bottle and repeat the color they named it. "This is your skin tone. You are the color of _____."

Variation: For Families with White Children

For this variation, show your child shades of brown and then repeat steps 1 and 2 of the skin-tone paint activity. When arriving at step 3, ask your child if the color brown they've made matches any brown shades they see around them. When arriving at step 4, ask, "What color would you call this?" Then label the bottle and repeat the color they named it.

Remember: We strongly recommend moving *away* from associating browns with food. If the child makes the association on their own, naturally work with the child to introduce other non-edible names. We want to move away from likening black and brown skin tones with consumption or fetishization.

Making Skin-Tone Playdough

For families with children ages four to seven years old

Having honest and inclusive skin-tone representation in toys, figures, and dolls can be greatly affirming for your children. Together, you and your children can create skin-tone playdough of multiple shades. They can use this playdough to re-create storybook characters, their classmates, family members, and neighbors.

- 2 cups all-purpose flour
- ¾ cup table salt
- 4 teaspoons cream of tartar
- 2 cups lukewarm water
- 2 tablespoons avocado oil
- 1 gallon-sized bag
- 4 quart-sized bags
- Food coloring (skin-toned)

1. In a large pot, stir the flour, salt, and cream of tartar together, then add the water and oil.
2. Cook over medium heat, stirring constantly, until the dough has thickened and begins to form a ball.
3. Remove from heat and then place inside a bowl or gallon-sized bag.
4. Allow to cool slightly, then knead until smooth.
5. Divide the dough into four balls and place each ball in a quart-sized bag.
6. Add skin-tone food coloring. Knead the dough, keeping it inside the bag; otherwise it will stain your hands.
7. Store the playdough inside the bags to keep soft. If stored properly, it will keep soft for up to three months.

*Disclaimer: This dough is NOT taste-safe and should not be consumed by children or pets.

Note: There are several skin-tone playdough recipes circling the internet that require food items—most often cocoa powder—to create the color brown. We strongly recommend moving away from associating browns with chocolate and food. If the child makes the association on their own, work to introduce the child to other, non-edible associations. We want to avoid linking black and brown skin tones with consumption or fetishization.

Exploring and Describing Skin Tones

For families with children ages two to seven years old

Young children are learning their mother tongue(s) and are so excited to communicate with us. One- and two-year-olds are mimicking sounds, expressing a few words and phrases, and identifying themselves using "me" and "my" pronouns. Children as young as three begin to show an interest in writing; shortly afterward, reading begins. As your children start to learn color names, don't skip over the color brown. In fact, it was one of the first colors I introduced in my home. We can help our children notice the richness of browns and blacks to understand that brown is beautiful.

Welcome conversations to discuss and recenter Black and brown skin tones by using rich language. Start with the basic colors:

- Black
- Brown
- Beige
- Ivory

Then, add modifiers:

- Dark, deep, rich, cool
- Warm, medium, tan
- Fair, light, pale

After reading a picture book together or watching a show, discuss the characters with your child. "Which color matches his color?" "What color would you call this?"

Explore browns in nature and draw attention to the names:

- Red clay brown
- Beach sand brown
- Desert sand brown
- Pinecone brown
- Acorn brown
- Mahogany brown
- Walnut brown
- Chestnut brown
- Ebony brown

Affirming Different Hair Textures

For families with children ages two to five years old. Variations are detailed.

There have been many stories about Black people having their hair touched without their consent. More often than not, the cause of this lack of awareness and respect by those who do so has to do with a lack of exposure to bodies different from theirs. Discussions about diversity as well as practices of consent early on will be vital to prevent these moments of othering.

Two-year-olds: Two-year-olds are curious about hair texture. It's oftentimes one of the first things they touch when exploring a new person. Three- and four-year-olds want to know how they got their hair: "Did I get my hair from Mommy or Daddy?" They might wonder how much their hair is going to change, how long it will grow.

Parents can start watching for verbal expressions of prejudice around three and four years old. Children might laugh at another child's hairstyle or say, "They have crazy hair." It's important to always disrupt these comments as soon as possible (please see "phrases to disrupt" on page 103 for some ideas). By the time children are five, they can begin to understand scientific explanations about hair as well as eye shapes, eye colors, and skin tones.

When they're organically exploring hair textures, model asking for consent: "Ms. Becky, can Remi touch your hair?" Use rich language to describe the hair color and texture to your child, focusing on giving the power of identification to the person your child is curious about: "Ms. Becky, how do you describe your hair?"

Three- and four-year-olds: Your child can begin to care for their hair independently at this age. Depending on the texture of hair and its development, this might mean putting their bonnet on at night, putting hair oil in a small spray bottle and spraying their scalp, helping to prepare for hair braiding, brushing their hair with a child-sized hairbrush, or putting small alligator clips in their hair. It's a good idea to have a small mirror they can use afterward to see themselves. Have a conversation with your child describing their hair: *my hair is dark brown, my hair is really curly, my hair has four braids, my hair is in two pigtails, my hair is straight,* etc. You can convey that just like how your child cares for their hair, others care for their hair, too, even if it looks and feels different from theirs.

Five-year-olds: Children can continue to learn how to take care of their hair by using hair mannequins. Training mannequins come in a wide variety of styles, so we can introduce them to other hair textures and styles, too. As our children have fun spraying the hair with water, brushing, combing, and clipping the hair, we should model accurate language for hair textures and styles. When they're ready, my children work with my partner to cut the hair using either safety scissors or clippers. We should work on building awareness, admiration, and respect during this exercise.

Painting Handprints

For families with children ages three to five years old

1. Trace your and your child's handprints.
2. Make skin-tone paint to color in your handprints (see page 84).
3. Describe your handprints and their shades using rich language.
4. Ask, "How have your hands helped you to accomplish a goal lately?"

Introducing Racialized Identities and Language

For families with children ages six to twelve years old. Variations are detailed.

For this exercise, research different types of maps with your children to reference. Then, refer to the example language provided below to discuss migration, racialized identities, and melanin.

What you'll need:

1. Map showing the ultraviolet light by latitudes
2. Migration map

Example language for six- to nine-year-olds

"About two hundred thousand years ago, modern humans only existed in Africa, then groups slowly began to migrate to other continents. What's one thing we know about Africa based on looking at the latitude map? Africa is hot! The red shows direct sunlight. Our human ancestors experienced the sun's powerful ultraviolet radiation. But don't worry, they had a lot of melanin to help protect their skin, which acts as a natural protectant from the sun. Melanin are special cells within the skin that contain the most obvious pigments (colors). Here's the same map with just the color brown. Our ancestors started in Africa and migrated. As groups migrated away from the equator, those groups had to lose some of their melanin sunscreen and became lighter in color due to the weaker sunlight. All humans have melanin. Your genes from your parents and grandparents will control how much melanin you receive, but your environment also plays a part. The more melanin, the darker the skin. The less melanin, the lighter the skin. And that's why we have different skin colors. While this touches on 'race,' it doesn't explain why we have racism. That's another conversation."

Follow-up activities after this conversation:

1. Identify continents on the map.
2. Continue to clarify that we're all descendants of people from Africa.
3. Print out a blackline master of the skin-tone map and paint the map using skin-tone paint.

Example language for ten-year-olds and up

"Our story begins with migration from Africa. Migration refers to the movement of people around Earth. Since the earliest of times, people have migrated for three main reasons: (1) to access natural resources, (2) to improve their quality of life, and (3) the need to relocate due to war, conquest, and/or invasion. We can add climate change and disasters to the list, too. Our migration story has contributed to the physical diversity in humans today.

"According to the Merriam-Webster dictionary, a species is 'a group of similar living things that ranks below the genus in scientific classification and is made up of individuals able to produce offspring with one another. [For example,] the one-humped camel is a different species from the two-humped camel.'[10] Modern humans are a part of the same species because we can reproduce with any human being. There's only one human species alive today; everyone belongs to modern humans. While this touches on 'race,' it doesn't explain why we have racism. How racism was created and continues to divide people is another conversation."

After this discussion, talk with your child about your ancestral/migration history.

Part Two started our journey in raising antiracist children to love their bodies and value all bodies. As you explore race, health, body-positivity, anti-sexism, and self-love with your antiracist skills, you should constantly recenter people of the global majority, looking for discriminatory systems at play, and creating space for conversations to happen with your family. Together, your family is forging a more just world.

To incorporate these conversations into daily happenings, normalize talking about your child's identity and your identity. You'll find your flow; the conversations will become natural because you both will have the shared language and vocabulary to discuss skin tones, hair textures, body sizes, abilities, and stereotypes. Don't worry about finishing a practice perfectly; instead think about progressing through the practices together. The goal is to develop your child's sense of agency, help them learn to set and respect boundaries, and empower them to think about the social norms they will follow and which ones to challenge. This will require lots of mistakes, allowing our children to handle the natural consequences that will arise, and responding with, "What do you need from me?" Most important, when our children experience feelings of guilt or even shame, we can always respond with, "I love you anyway . . ." The way you respond to your children in the tough times will become their inner voice later in life.

We hope you and your children have learned a bit more about how to foster healthy and happy relationships with your bodies, especially regarding race, body-positivity, feminism, and self-love. We encourage you to continue these practices and even make some of your own.

radical minds

The world watched George Floyd's murder and then watched multiple systems collude for injustice over his death, and *that*, my friend, is racism. Racism is not some idea or abstract concept, it has real consequences. Thanks to one brave teenager, Darnella Frazier, who refused to stop recording, we were all forced to bear witness to the violence.

I don't think anyone was prepared to discuss what was witnessed. Rightfully, one of the loudest questions became: "How do I talk with my child about this?" Parenting partners struggled to discuss the police department's absolute failure to protect and serve. Unsure of how much to say, what's developmentally appropriate to communicate, and what the *right* thing to say is weighs on parents across the nation.

Part Three offers parenting partners the tool of liberating language. Antiracist parenting leans into the feelings of discomfort and develops a practice of questioning, wondering, and reflecting. This part will explore the language of racial justice and white domination. It will also offer the tools to build a home rooted in justice, as well as an invitation to reimagine how tending to your mental health can be liberating, too.

Liberating Language

For infants through preschoolers, I use *unfair* as an umbrella term to describe prejudice, group discrimination, policies, laws, and anything else discriminatory our society has normalized. I use the term *fair* to describe the actions we take to provide the resources and care people need. It's easier to approach these topics from this familiar angle than introducing terms such as *bias*, *discrimination*, and *prejudice* at this age.

Fairness is not the same as equality. Equality is the goal, while fairness is "the work" (a set of actions) we practice in hopes of achieving it. Equality won't ever get us there. Antiracism then becomes the journey, with equality as a destination.

While fairness is a complex idea for people, in my experience children have a strong internal compass of fairness. As antiracist parents, we should emphasize that fairness is about people receiving what they need. When you begin having necessary conversations about inequality, discrimination, and racism with your young child, you can start with these words in order to best approach the subject.

For children six to nine years old, we can begin introducing the language of racial justice. *Fairness* evolves into *justice* and *unfairness* evolves into more specific language we commit to memory. Each definition should be explicitly taught and used frequently in conversations in order to help children truly grasp their meaning and their context.

1. **Prejudice**—having opinions or ideas about a person without actually knowing them.
2. **Stereotype**—an attitude, belief, feeling, or assumption about a person based on their social identity that's widespread and socially

accepted; stereotypes have negative effects because they support institutionalized oppression by validating oversimplified beliefs that aren't based on facts.

3. **Discrimination**—when people act on those negative opinions, assumptions, or attitudes (prejudices). It's when we deny individuals or groups of people fair treatment.

4. **Racism**—personal prejudice + systemic misuse and abuse of power. Two other acceptable and accurate definitions of racism are: (1) "Racism is prejudice against someone because of their race, and when those views are reinforced by systems of power"[1] and (2) "A system of advantage based on race."[2]

For children ten to thirteen years old, language becomes much more expansive, creative, and critical. Embrace this creativity and your adolescents' natural critical thinking skills to enjoy the language of racial justice. Above all, adopt language that humanizes the person and places the blame on the discriminatory system.

Here's the language I use with my children to develop their critical thinking skills, encourage dialogue, and interrupt misconceptions as they happen:

1. **When I hear my children repeat a stereotype, I call it out: "You're repeating a stereotype."** I want to make it clear that there's no such thing as a positive stereotype. All stereotypes come at the expense of seeing a group of people as a monolithic group, denying their humanity, individuality, creativity, and imagination. More often than not, racial stereotypes are rooted in the belief that race is biological and genetic. When we hear children reference stereotypes, it's important to interrupt them. I ask my own children: "How does this stereotype hurt or harm the community? How does it prevent us from seeing the community in reality?" Consider asking your children (and yourself) the same questions.

2. **When I hear my children inaccurately refer to systemic prejudice as *mean*, I want to impress upon them the gravity of the situation.** Discrimination is easily defined as prejudice plus action, so when our children notice unfair or racist policies and regulations in place, we can introduce the idea of discrimination. When we take prejudiced thoughts, ideas, and emotions and put them into action, that's discrimination. This action can happen both interpersonally (one-on-one) and in a group. When backed by policies or laws, it's institutionalized discrimination. Any group can experience discrimination: women experience workplace discrimination, people who breastfeed experience breastfeeding discrimination, the disabled community experiences accessibility discrimination, the LGBTQ+ community experiences health-care discrimination, and so on.

3. **When I hear kids denying something is racist (or inaccurately dubbing something as racist), I want to make them conscious of the power dynamics at play.** In today's covert racist world, we must do a bit more unpacking with our children to connect how racism is at play. We know it's racism when:

   a. a person of the global majority tells us it's racism. Period.
   b. there are race-based outcomes. Period.
   c. there is a historical pattern that's disproportionately affecting people of the global majority. Period.

Last but not least, an honest question I always receive from children is, "Can white people experience racism?" My answer? No. Racism by definition needs to be backed by systems and institutions, and there aren't any groups of the global majority who hold systemic power in the United States. We'll go more into this in the next section.

Noticing Racism versus Being Mean

"That's racist!"

This is a common statement young people make when practicing calling out discrimination. Before responding, quickly recall your family's definition of racism (personal prejudice + the systemic misuse and abuse of power by institutions).

If what they're pointing out *is* racist, affirm your child. "Yes. I agree." Then challenge them further for understanding: "Can you tell me how that is prejudice plus power?" or "Can you identify who's benefiting from this racism and what systems are supporting it?" We should always think about the systems supporting injustice, and we should always encourage our children to think about them, too.

Most important, support your child in disrupting racism by asking, "What can you do to create change?" Antiracism goes beyond identifying racism; we all must work toward solutions to counteract it. By inviting your child to think critically and creatively about ways they can be a catalyst for change, you plant the seeds of proactive, committed action.

Now, what should you do if what your child identifies isn't racism? If it's *not* racism, affirm they're practicing calling it out: "I see you're practicing finding racism." Then, ask them an open question:

1. "What made you think it was racist?"
2. "Could you tell me more?"
3. "What's the power dynamic or system being used?"

It's important to remind our children that we do live in a racist society and systemic racism is difficult to identify. If it was another form of systemic oppression or discrimination, then correct it. "Oh. That's actually sexism, because . . ."

If your child is calling out meanness (an individual act that was rude), correctly identify the behavior as being rude, mean, or unkind so the other child can take the right action. This is especially true for white children who use the term *racist* to mean an insult. It's imperative to correct this behavior; otherwise, it clouds their understanding of the psychological toll and discrimination people of the global majority experience because of racism. Finally, always remind our children that calling someone a racist is not a slur or an insult. It's a label identifying a system of advantage so we can dismantle it.

Will you take a deep breath before this next sentence?

Children of the global majority experience systemic racism and also interpersonal racism, and the latter is coming from their white peers. If you're the parent of a white child, pay special attention to the following points:

1. If your child was called racist, help them understand it's not an attack on their humanity, but a behavior that can and should be changed for their own benefit.
2. Inform them that they can choose to continue the behavior or choose an antiracist behavior.
3. If they do choose a different behavior, support your child in understanding their actions and seek ways to repair harm. Accountability and change are wonderful, important things, so encouraging children to take responsibility is imperative.
4. If they choose to continue their racist behavior, support your child in trying to understand their actions, then seek further support from your parenting partners, school personnel, and counselors. Remember, this will be a constant conversation.

Our children will notice our racist ways or the ways we uphold racism (for families of the global majority), too. Be prepared for them to hold us accountable; the steps above apply to us, as well.

Here's an example of my own: My family and I were running

behind (per usual), so I yelled, "Let's go, we have to run to the grocery store and get back as soon as possible." As we shuffled out of the house, Carter struggled to find a mask he wanted to wear (this was during the COVID-19 pandemic).

"It's not a fashion show," I said. "Just grab one and let's go." Carter complied, but was upset. On the way to the grocery store, I could tell he was frustrated. I asked him to help me understand the issue. He quickly replied, "This mask is racist! I don't want to wear it in the grocery store."

I looked over and saw it was a Chicago Blackhawks mask that was donated to our family when COVID-19 first hit. Even though I knew the mascot was a harmful stereotype, I didn't take actions to disrupt it by immediately throwing it away.

When we work to build awareness and analysis with our children, it's not just to give truth to the world, it's to give the people in their circle truth, too. At this moment, my child was telling me a mask we have is racist and he did not want to uphold racism by associating with it. While I made a mistake initially, I invited him to tell me how he was feeling and how I could do better.

Addressing Prejudice, Stereotypes, and Biased Language

I was standing in line for coffee one day, deliberating over which pastry to order, when a seven-year-old in line attempted to whisper, "Her skirt is too short." The mom's silence highlighted her embarrassment. The teenager standing ahead of them, wearing the skirt, looked even more humiliated. I took a deep breath and proudly said, "They chose to wear what makes them feel good. Just like you chose to wear your outfit today." When we begin to listen to our children—*really* listen—we'll hear them make observations that need to be interrupted and redirected. It's helpful to categorize your children's statements as curious questions or inaccurate statements. "Mommies can't be in wheelchairs" or "Black people are bad" are inaccurate statements. Oftentimes, our first inclination as caregivers when our child says something rooted in prejudice is to shut it down as fast as possible. If we're in public, we might give an awkward smile and talk through our teeth or avoid responding to their claim altogether. But what message are we sending children when we do this? Next time, communicate clearly, tell your truth, and partner with your child to draw a more accurate conclusion.

Addressing Inaccurate Statements

For parents and caregivers

When our children put their shoes on the wrong feet, we might ask, "Do your shoes feel uncomfortable? Let me help you." If our children declare, "Two plus three equals seven," we respond with, "Not quite. Can you try again?" Our responses should be no different when correcting our children's misconceptions about people. Instead, SHARE in the learning with children. Prejudice is learned, so it can be unlearned.

> **S:** Say something right away
> **H:** Help them to understand
> **A:** Ask for help
> **R:** Repair the harm
> **E:** Embrace critical conversations

An example of an incorrect statement: "Ew. Her food is weird. I don't want to sit by her."

S: Immediately say something to your child and reframe their statement to bring them into the conversation: "Macy, that's not true. Her food is different. I wonder who made her lunch?"

H: Help your child see differences as something to enjoy, explore, and appreciate. Think about a book you could read together, a takeout restaurant to order from, or a food fair you could try.

A: Ask for help. Don't be afraid to ask for help from your parenting partners, your child's teacher, and friends. Create connection by introducing yourself to those in the community your child made the incorrect statement about. Diversify your and your child's universe and make cross-cultural friendships.

R: If your child said something to another person, check on the other child in the moment: "Hi. I heard what Macy said to you. How are you feeling?"

E: Embrace the critical conversation. Depending on what your child said, ask to speak to their grown-up so you can loop the grown-up into the conversation. With this act of inclusion of your community members, you're modeling healthy and collaborative critical conversations for your child. Your child can then best repair any harm with those who experienced it, but also, your child (and you) can create authentic relationships. Through addressing the situation versus ignoring it, we can encourage education, healing, and friendships, and discourage shame, avoidance, and perpetuation.

Choosing Family Values

As an antiracist parent, I know that the values I hold play a key role in the decisions I make for my family and for who my children will become. Early in our antiracist journey, I learned about the white domination characteristics developed by Tema Okun and Daniel Buford.[3] The fifteen characteristics they've outlined (perfectionism, sense of urgency, defensiveness, quantity over quality, worship of the written word, only one right way, paternalism, either/or thinking, power hoarding, fear of open conflict, individualism, I'm the only one, progress is bigger, objectivity, and right to comfort) show up in organizations, boardrooms, classrooms, and as I quickly learned, in our homes, too. The cycle of racism is passed generation to generation through these invisible values.

I've invited my friends Katie and Kerry to share how they're disrupting three of the white domination characteristics. This is important for a variety of reasons. In order to be antiracists, we must address white domination within ourselves and our families. Keep in mind that only you can really know and identify how these characteristics are shared, learned, and passed generation to generation in your family. My hope is that Katie and Kerry's modeling will set you in the right direction to unpack each of the characteristics within yourself.

One language difference to note here is that Katie and Kerry prefer the term *folx* to *folks* as an act of explicit gender-inclusion. Adding the "x" forces the gender-binary to be confronted and challenged. There are many different takes on this term and its spelling, and we're all invited to explore how we're consciously thinking and using language.

The Manifestation of White Domination Culture in Our Home

For white families

This book is filled with the labor, experiences, and expertise of adults of the global majority centering antiracism and liberation in their relationships with children. While our voices stand alongside the authors of this book, we want to explicitly dismantle the notion that white folx, including us, are able to claim "expertise" in antiracist work. Instead of expertise, we aim to center community and compassionate accountability for ourselves and other white adults.

We strive each day, and in each moment, to become the antiracist white adults we desperately needed as children. We know we cannot do this work alone—we must reject the lies that white domination culture teaches us about individualism and exceptionalism. We know that while addressing the manifestations of white domination culture within ourselves is crucial, we must always have our eyes on the systemic, material realities of racism. To do that, we must move beyond ourselves as individuals, and into the creation of explicitly antiracist community with other white folx. As white adults, we've been socialized to believe we can get what we want faster if we go it alone. We want you to link arms with us, because no one can get to the world we're dreaming of alone.

THE WHITE DOMINATION CULTURE CHARACTERISTICS

Right to Comfort	Perfectionism	Sense of Urgency	Power Hoarding
Either/Or Thinking	Objectivity	Individualism	Only One Right Way
Quantity over Quality	Fear of Open Conflict	Paternalism	I'm the Only One
Defensiveness	Worship of the Written Word	Progress Is Bigger, More	

For further reading, please see "White Supremacy Culture" by Tema Okun.[4]

How Can White Adults Disrupt White Domination with White Children?

Some folks believe antiracist work is separate from their day-to-day interactions with one another, or that antiracist work is really glorified "self-betterment" done in small book clubs, or through continuous consumption of workshops. We want to challenge those inclinations and think about antiracism as a series of actions that happen moment-to-moment throughout every aspect of our lives. The cycle of conscious reflection and action, as Lilia Monzó teaches, does not only apply to big decisions like interrupting racist acts in the moment or arriving at a protest—it also shows up in how we talk about our bodies, how we define success, and how we speak to ourselves when we make a mistake.

Our homes are not exempt from the systems of domination that dictate social life in the United States. Oftentimes, they mirror, replicate, and uphold the power dynamics that define white domination culture, patriarchy, cissexism, and other dynamics of domination. They can also be places of radical reimagining, where we work in community within our most intimate relationships with our partners, children, and family members to uproot white domination culture.

Reimaging an antiracist white racial identity dedicated to liberation is more than teaching children facts about racism. It's a commitment we must embody and model. It requires rebuilding relationships with the other white people in our and our children's lives. Oftentimes it can feel more difficult to engage in explicitly antiracist conversations with adults (even those who we're closest to) than with children. Children notice this. Children notice when we tense up at a racialized remark and hold our tongues. They notice if there are adults in their lives who talk to them about antiracism behind closed doors so as not to upset other white adults. They notice when the conversations of the adults around them uphold white silence. And it's these patterns of silence and conflict avoidance that will begin to shape their relationship with either antiracist action or compliant inaction.

This practice will ask you to consider:

- How has white domination culture shown up in the daily interactions within your home sphere (including any adults who share relationships with children)?
- How have you previously responded when white domination has shown up in you, your children, or your personal world?
- What would it look and sound like to disrupt patterns of white domination culture when they show up in ways that don't reinforce domination?

Activity Part 1: Parent/Caregiver Reflection (10–15 minutes)

White domination culture is most often *not* explicitly taught to children, and yet this system of domination continues to reinforce itself generation after generation. White domination culture dominates social and political relations and systems in the United States, and it's inevitable that we'll continue to internalize messages that uphold the centrality of whiteness. The clearer we can become about where and how we ourselves have absorbed and continue to absorb these messages, the more effectively we can disrupt the same process for our children.

For this reflection, we invite you to consider where and how you first internalized messages about the characteristics of white domination culture. After familiarizing yourself with the characteristics of white supremacy culture,[5] find a space that will support your reflection. Take a moment to check in with your body. Notice the physical sensations, emotions, and thoughts present in this moment. Feel free to use the writing space below to capture your wonderings.

Question: When reading the list of white domination culture characteristics, are there any I feel an embodied or physical reaction to? Do I feel tightening, constriction, heat, tension, pain, or even emptiness when imagining these characteristics in myself?

Select one characteristic that feels most resonant for you, then proceed with the rest of this reflection:

* Where in your life can you recall learning and internalizing this characteristic?
* Where or with whom did you receive messaging around this characteristic?
* How was this characteristic upheld as the norm, or the most desired behavior?
* How can you create space to hold yourself accountable to heal from and disrupt this messaging?

_____

_____

_____

_____

_____

_____

Part 2: Finding Daily Opportunities to Disrupt White Domination Culture

This practice centers the reality that antiracism is not what we post to social media or scribble on a protest sign, but rather is found in the decisions, conversations, and behaviors we make and model each day. As we recognize our own role in upholding and perpetuating these systems of dominance, we must also keep in mind that we're only responsible for some aspects of our children's socialization. We're one of the many teachers that they'll encounter in their lives. Our children will encounter many influences that will impact their racial identity development, from their educators in school to the media they consume. Our goal isn't to strive for perfection—we know that even with our best and most earnest efforts our children will still absorb racist messaging. Our goal is to create a family culture that actively challenges these messages and models open and honest communication about race, racism, and white domination. While the examples here focus on disrupting these patterns in our relationships with children, remember that it's equally important to be establishing this antiracist culture with the other adults in our lives as well.

For this practice, we'll focus on several of the characteristics of white domination culture. When looking at each characteristic, we will:

- Share personal anecdotes that illustrate how we're still learners present on our own antiracist journeys.
- Provide examples of how each of these characteristics could manifest in white children while also offering humanizing ways to challenge them that center antiracism.

Because we've been taught that only bad people can enact racism, it can be difficult to acknowledge patterns of white domination culture in ourselves and those we love. As you read how these characteristics may manifest in our children, you may experience discomfort at the thought of seeing or experiencing these very common and typical behaviors in the children in your lives. Remember, this isn't about labeling white children as white supremacists. We do not believe that most children are purposefully enacting racism. We also know that white children learn to access power and exert dominance over others through their whiteness. How we disrupt these common behaviors will model for our children how we can develop antiracist racial identities, and collectively choose to interact and move through the world in more loving, humanizing, and radically disruptive ways.

Characteristic 1: Perfectionism

People tend to think that perfection will lead to quality and excellence, but that isn't really the case. They strive for perfection in order to prove their value to those who hold power, since they're the ones setting the standards. Those in power define and demand perfection, but *perfectionism is a construct*. We acknowledge these characteristics aren't necessarily inherently bad, but these characteristics are always in service to current power structures. These are tools to preserve the status quo. Perfectionism encourages folks to prove their value in service of the current power structures at play. It directly affects people of the global majority when it's denying people access, and being used to justify exclusion, and/or telling them to "just try harder." At the end of the day, white domination is benefited by perfectionism because perfectionism preserves power and the status quo: society's ideal of perfect is linked to whiteness, thinness, being educated, and masculinity, so when one doesn't meet those standards of perfectionism, people of the GM are forced to try to fit into a mold they will never (and should never have to) fit into.

You can, however, decide what excellence is for you. You can set that goal and that standard; you don't have to judge yourself against some predetermined perfect ideal.

Katie shares: No one ever told me I had to be perfect. In fact, I'm sure the adults in my life lovingly told me it was okay to make mistakes, and that no one does everything perfectly all of the time. And yet, I struggle deeply with tying my self-worth to my ability to perform tasks as perfectly as possible. Teasing out how I learned this commitment to a narrow definition of perfectionism has been a complicated task—one that's required a great deal of compassion for my parents and for myself. I remember these cups that we used to eat chili out of. They were stoneware, speckled gray and brown, with curving writing on them that read "home sweet home." There were four, one for each of us. One day, while washing one of those cups, it slipped from my hands, breaking in the sink. I remember this immediate feeling of dread. I carefully gathered all of the pieces, dried them, and then crept out to my father's supply drawer in the garage to find superglue. I snuck back into my room, then waited until late at night to glue the pieces together as perfectly as I could. I returned the cup to the shelf, praying no one would notice.

Regardless of how my parents may have responded in reality, I had internalized the message that making mistakes was unacceptable. I had witnessed my parents' frustrations with their own mistakes—yelling or throwing their hands up when they broke something.

HOW THIS CHARACTERISTIC MIGHT MANIFEST IN . . .

Children	Adults
• Afraid to share or show that they have broken something • Afraid to share a grade on an assignment or assessment • Wanting to quit or give up a given activity if they cannot perform "perfectly" • Wanting to avoid trying new tasks altogether • Expressing frustration with siblings or peers who are not performing a task in the "right" way • Profusely or constantly apologizing when there is no transgression	• Cursing, yelling when they break something or make a mistake • Negative self-talk—"I can't believe I did that, I'm such a mess." • Not engaging in activities such as singing, dancing, or art because of a narrative of "not being good" at them • Criticizing one's body—"I'm so fat. I can't eat that because I won't fit into my jeans." This might also look like avoiding photos because of worries about appearance. • Voicing judgment about people's character when they are not living up to our personal values or expectations

When you hear **"Please don't be mad! I broke or lost _____"** or **"Please don't tell Mom/Dad I had an accident!"** . . .

PAUSE. Ensure you're grounded and calm. This is essential because our messaging is wrapped up in our body language and our tone. Then, let them share what happened, and make space for their feelings while stating that mistakes are part of being a human. Offer: **"I hear you. Let's clean/try to fix it. Humans make mistakes. Since making mistakes is**

part of who we are, we don't have to be afraid when it happens." When we model that making mistakes and being mistakes are not the same thing, mistakes become essential parts of humanity—something we all have in common—and lose their power over us.

Here's an important thing to keep in mind: you won't teach your children perfect antiracism, you won't be a perfect antiracist, or a perfect parent for that matter. Your children won't be perfect; no one is. We're human: beautifully flawed beings.

Characteristic 2: Power Hoarding

Kerry shares: My daughter Olivia loves to play with her friends. She shares often about how happy they make her and how she wishes they were together every day. At the moment, she is an only child at home and with her father and myself, doesn't seem to have much resistance to sharing . . . even the last bite of her favorite snacks. When she visits a friend's house, she expects them to willingly give up whatever toys or materials she wants in a moment and will look to me to support her understanding that "they're not sharing and not being a good friend." During our last visit with her friend Ben, I watched this conflict play out over a shiny blue Hot Wheels car. When Ben did not respond to Olivia's demands, he was met with tears, a scream, and a "sharing is caring" proclamation. She asked me to intervene to get Ben to release the car. The room was filled with toys, including a bucket of cars of all sizes. Olivia, while capable of sharing and spreading resources, internalized an entitlement to other people's things and associated their reluctance or refusal to acquiesce to her as being "bad." Despite our modeling and practicing sharing in our home, Olivia has a belief that in order to be a "good friend," someone is supposed to lose or give up what she wants. I could see here that trite phrases like "take turns" or "sharing is caring" do not make space for children to experience all of the real emotions that come with redistributing power and materials.

HOW THIS CHARACTERISTIC MIGHT MANIFEST IN . . .

Children	Adults
• Expressing and/or exhibiting entitlement to space, materials, time before others • Stating they are "the best" at something without honoring others' gifts • Insisting on being "in charge" or setting "the rules" in different settings or circumstances (projects, teams, games, etc.) without acknowledging the contributions of others • Pressuring peers to "prove" their friendship or loyalty while fearing losing relationships or that they may not have enough friendships • "You can't play with us because . . ." "you're a boy/you're not wearing pink/you have curly hair"	• Demanding to speak to the manager or person in power when your desires or expectations are not met • Taking advantage of financial assistance or programs when you hold economic privilege • Leveraging connections and resources to ensure a child has access to elite schools, extracurriculars, or jobs • Sharing job, board service, presentation opportunities only with friends and family • Campaigning for leadership positions in organizations (particularly those led by or composed mostly of people of the global majority) because of one's expertise, rather than contributing while following others' leadership

When you're at a playground or communal space and hear, **"Too bad, we were here first!"** or when you watch your child(ren) gather up all the materials/toys in a space . . .

PAUSE. I often jump into these situations too quickly before allowing space for my child to make a different choice or receive feedback from any other person in this situation.

Then offer: **"I can see/hear you're excited to play, but this space/ these things are for all friends. We need to make a choice that lets everyone have space/things to play with. What can you try instead?"** Stand firmly on the reality that *all* people and *all* materials are for the community.

Our society would have us believe that due to our hard work and success, we've earned and are entitled to certain spoils. Meritocracy sells the lie that feeds entitlement: that you're meant to have time, space, titles, money, success, jobs, and attention because you've "earned it." When we center meritocracy, we lose the realities of living within a system of white domination that manipulates all structures to keep white folx in positions of power. The more we embrace the nuance of sharing and power, the more our children can begin to see that while we encourage them to be generous with their resources, they're not entitled to the resources of others.

Characteristic 3: Fear of Open Conflict

Katie shares: I was three years old with loose blond curls tucked behind my ears and a pair of pink Western boots. Pink like my cheeks and my skin. My mom and I stood, eagerly waiting to check into school for the day. Looking at the Black man in front of us, I excitedly inquired, "Are you Kiana's dad?" The man turned, a smile on his face, and said, "Yes, I am. Why do you ask?"

A deep red blush spread across my mother's cheeks; her body tightened. I could feel the heat radiating off her; she knew what I was going to say next. "Well, you have the same brown skin she does." Without missing a beat, he replied, "I do! It runs in my family." Another smile, a wave, and then his exit.

"Katie, we don't ask people questions like that," my mom whispered, her voice laced with embarrassment. In that moment, I learned that there's something wrong about noticing someone's brown skin. I learned that there are questions we don't ask, and that I needed to keep my lips sealed. Why, I wasn't sure. This moment was not explicitly one of conflict—but my mom anticipated the discomfort or tension that could emerge as a result of my question. The expert maneuvering she did to avoid that potential conflict has been deeply ingrained into me—and is something that I continue to unlearn.

HOW THIS CHARACTERISTIC MIGHT MANIFEST IN . . .

Children	Adults
• Fearing speaking up for themselves to peers or to adults who have transgressed boundaries • Being coached through "if you do not have anything nice to say, say nothing" • Being encouraged to "turn the other cheek" rather than express a boundary • Worrying engaging in conflict will alienate friends or adults in their worlds • Reluctantly allow an adult to give them hugs, kisses, or physical contact because adults expect it	• Avoiding talking to one's partner, family, or friends when a racist incident occurs • Avoiding addressing boundary transgressions for fear of rocking the boat • Even in jest, encouraging children to keep activities secret. "Don't tell [adult] that we had ice cream tonight. That's just between us." • Handling adult conflict behind closed doors and not modeling respectful disagreement • Maintaining a "we don't talk about religion or politics" at the dinner table (or the office, or the place of worship, or the playground) policy

When you're with your family and hear another adult share a dehumanizing comment in proximity to your children . . .

PAUSE. The first moment of engagement needs to be done by the fellow adult. We DO NOT have the option to not engage. The complicity of our inaction will send a message to our children, regardless of the words or conversations we've had with them prior to this moment. There are multiple ways to engage here, depending on your conflict style and the other adult's conflict style. Holding boundaries here is firm, necessary, and compassionate.

Offer, **"I just need to say, that comment/joke made me very uncomfortable and isn't acceptable. I care too much about you to let you believe that comment was an 'okay' thing to say."** Then, offer space to have a deeper conversation if your boundaries (and the context) allow for it.

When you have a moment with your child, center their experience of the exchange with these call-ins:

"How did it make you feel when you heard that comment?"

"What do you think about that comment?"

"Next time, what would you say to (adult) if you heard that?"

After allowing space for their processing, remind them that we share the responsibility to everyone in our community to make choices that humanize everyone. You and your child are partners in creating spaces and a world where addressing dehumanizing and racialized harm are the norm, not the exception.

Disrupting manifestations of this characteristic begins with our interactions with other adults. We can model firm boundary setting, engagement in uncomfortable conversations, and how to directly address conflict when it shows up. We can model daily engagement in discussions and actions that address racism. We can also speak candidly about how we feel nervous, anxious, or uncomfortable when having these conversations, and those feelings are typical. This way, children don't expect conflict to always be easy or simple to manage, but they also learn the importance of continuing to show up even when it might feel difficult.

—Katie and Kerry

Researching Antiracist Abolitionists

For families with white children ages nine and older

When I set out to research white American antiracist abolitionists, I wanted to uplift and recover white antiracists who specifically sought out cross-racial coalition. With the activity, I sought the inspiration of folx who centered humanization, rather than intellectualism, in their antiracism. I've learned from Britt that one of the reasons why we haven't solved racism is because we're too concerned about intellectualizing it: reading books, learning the vocabulary, and looking the part, instead of actual healing from our legacy of racism.

The history and legacy of white folx in what became the United States is one of domination, violence, and erasure. We've heard lots of adults (including teachers) share concerns about "making students feel badly about being white." I want you to know: building a healthy antiracist white identity is possible. We know whiteness is a construct, one upheld in all of the systems that govern our lives. The histories of white folx acting toward disruption and liberation have been deliberately obscured in the education system. Just consider: While you were a student, which antiracist white co-conspirators did you learn about? Remember: White domination thrives on white solidarity. In my practice, you and the children in your life will do some digging to discover the reality of a legacy of white antiracist ancestors.

For this practice, the term *children* refers to white children. **This practice is meant to reclaim and model white antiracist ancestors for white children.** Before beginning this research project with your child-partners, you'll also need to establish definitions and understanding of the following: **racism**, **antiracism**, **whiteness**, and **abolitionists**.

Children are thoughtful and empowered partners when they have all the information they need. Start by creating shared language around the terms above. Aside from getting familiar with these terms in Part One of this book, you can also reference *This Book Is Anti-Racist* by Tiffany Jewell, *Refusing Racism: White Allies and the Struggle for Civil Rights* by Cynthia Stokes Brown, and *A Promise and a Way of Life: White Antiracist Activism* by Becky Thompson.

1. Now that you and the children have established a shared language, assemble resources to support your research.

   a. **Notice how textbooks might whitewash history.** Consider the abolitionist John Brown, for example: he sought armed, violent rebellion to destroy the institution of slavery. At no point did his teachings or writings center the humanity of Black folx toiling under slavery. One of the first people killed by Brown's band was a freed Black man who refused to listen to Brown's orders. Even in recounting the legacy of John Brown within textbooks, he's the central figure; the five Black abolitionists (including the only Black survivor of the raid on Harpers Ferry, Osborne Anderson) are not centered, or often, not even mentioned.[6] Remember: White antiracists and white abolitionists should work in solidarity with people of the global majority.

   b. While the Civil Rights Movement offers many examples of white antiracists, consider researching early abolitionist and antislavery groups founded even during the Colonial and Revolutionary periods. Make note to distinguish between allies who believed in the abolishment of slavery and co-conspirators who actually risked something to abolish slavery.

   c. Digital archives and digital history projects are incredibly invaluable for research. We've used the resources gathered by Lynn Burnett, as an example.[7]

   d. **Models, Not Saviors:** A final note when conducting this research. The purpose here is to rediscover white folx who made choices to disrupt white domination. If their choices and actions are placed on a pedestal, it centers them as saviors and makes their choices seem irreplicable, rather than inspirational. Use language that focuses on the choices these people made to the children, and that we, too, have choices to make. Remember, antiracism is found in our daily habits and choices.

2. Leveraging your research, develop a plan for integrating your new understanding of antiracist action into your life and into your community.

   a. Putting your learning into action, start with where you already have influence and connections (your neighborhood, school district, places where you spend or contribute money). Where can you take more deliberate and disruptive action?

   b. How can you be including your children in this work? You could, for example, role-play with your children how to interrupt racist comments and behavior they (and their classmates) experience at school.

   —Kerry LiBrando

Antiracist Values

The slow and deeply vulnerable process to unpack and analyze how the characteristics unintentionally show up in my parenting practice drove me to develop values rooted in love and justice. My chosen values resist my almost natural ability to avoid conflict, my desire to be the perfect parent with the right answers that has it all figured out. Instead, I seek authenticity, curiosity, collaboration, accountability, becoming, empowerment, and candor. I chose values that directly disrupt harmful dominant beliefs, support critical thinking, and allow our children to live out values of justice. My seven chosen values:

1. **Be Curious.** We grow when we seek new information to enhance our understanding of racism. We cultivate wonderings in our home and embrace our child's wonders, too. Our child is on their journey of learning and I am on my journey of unlearning and relearning. I will practice responding with curiosity rather than fear.

2. **Be Accountable.** Staying in a relationship with people calls for accountability. Every person has a role to play in making our community a just place, including myself. When I accept my responsibility, the relationship grows stronger and the work moves forward. Without shifting the blame, I will take responsibility for my actions.

3. **Be Empowered.** With a deep breath in, connect to my deepest hopes, values, and expectations. I will remember, I am the right person to disrupt and I have everything I need right now to start. I will look for ways I can contribute time and funds to my local mutual aid organizations, make a practice to grocery shop for our local food distribution site, or call our local school to find volunteer opportunities. I trust myself to do what is right and ask for the resources I need.

4. **Be Candid.** Discuss race and racism with my children, family

members, and friends. Avoiding the conversation only leads to inaccurate conclusions and feelings of guilt, shame, regret, and frustration. I will allow the truth to take up space and know my truth is a gift.

5. **Be Collaborative.** Collaboration requires each person to do their own work of learning, sharing, and working in partnership with one another. When my actions are focused on connection and justice, recentering will happen. I will amplify and work with historically underrepresented and underresourced groups.

6. **Be Becoming.** Acknowledging this information wasn't included in our K-12 education, in our birthing classes, or shared widely, so we'll always be on a journey. I'll rise to the everyday challenges and opportunities of antiracism because I love who I am becoming. I will honor who I was when I started and realize who I'm becoming.

7. **Be Authentic.** Live out your values by allowing your thoughts and actions to be in harmony with one another. I will experience the fullest of what my body has to offer: laughter, singing, and dancing. Above all, I will experience joy.

Embracing Conversations

A curious environment invites us to interrogate who we are, who we're becoming, and the experiences we've lived through. An empathetic environment allows us to live in that truth.

Our homes will center parts of us, our culture, and our history. Our homes can become places where the tough stuff is shared and, in return, met with empathy. Empathy allows us to hold two truths at the same time. It allows me to hold my reality and your experience by relating to a shared feeling, and this creates a meaningful connection.

"They told me I wasn't really Black."

"The teacher said I was going to hell for being gay."

When we practice empathy, we connect and build mutual relationships, which is an essential part of mental health. Ultimately, our home becomes a space where our children are embraced and valued.

At the same time, all children need curious and honest environments, too. A curious environment allows us to experience radical empathy—which is the heart of anti-bias and antiracism—and practice critical thinking. Curiosity allows us to work through our differences, to hold each other accountable (both the child and the adult), and to come to new understandings. When someone causes harm or experiences discrimination, it allows us to give and receive the truth as a gift. In order for empathy, curiosity, and candor to happen, parenting partners have to agree: we will embrace curious conversations and be willing to learn from each other.

Responding with Curiosity

Cobe started piano lessons last year. His piano teacher invited him to perform in the upcoming winter recital. One night, Cobe overheard his dad and myself talking about the upcoming piano recital. From his room he yelled, "I'm not doing that!"

I immediately asked Cobe to come to our room so he could respond with curiosity. "Ask me three questions about the piano recital before making a decision," I requested. His very first response was, "Mom, I don't even know what a piano recital is." Once he'd learned more, he decided to participate. After our discussion, I reminded him to respond with curiosity rather than fear. Watching him perform at his piano recital warmed my heart.

This small exchange shows one way we could respond with

curiosity rather than with silence or demands. Responding with curiosity also allows for the conversation to flow regardless of how much information we have or how uncomfortable I am by the question.

More ways to respond with curiosity:

1. "Who told you?"
2. "Where did you hear this?"
3. "Do you believe that to be true? Why?"
4. "Could you tell me more?"
5. "Show me . . ."
6. "I wonder why they would say that?"
7. "What are you curious about?"
8. "Who could we ask to find out more?"
9. "Where could we search to find out more?"
10. "What are three questions you have?"

Responding with Empathy

You might be driving to pick up groceries with your partner, on the walk home from school with our child, or sitting at the dinner table when all of a sudden your loved one shares:

"I'm fat!"
"I don't like the color of my brown!"
"They said I was acting white."

1. I might respond with: "Wow! I need to take a deep breath." This models pausing and taking deep breaths, which can reduce our elevated stress and allow us to better move through the discomfort.
2. When I'm looking to take the pain away by offering a quick fix, I remind myself to trust my silence—that my presence is enough—and say, "I'm here and listening."

3. I ask the person to share: "What emotion is showing up for you right now?" This allows me to tap into a time when I felt that same emotion.

4. At all costs, avoid saying, "Well, when I was in school . . ." Instead, try "I've been there, and that really hurts" or (to quote an example from Brené Brown) "It sounds like you're in a hard place now. Tell me more about it."

The Three Cs: Care for the Self, Our Neighbors, and the Environment

Care for Self

Now more than ever it's important for future generations to know that they deserve support in caring for themselves. This type of self-care dedication can go beyond rest; it can also include unpacking and healing through trauma. I've invited my coauthor, Tasha, to talk a bit about the intersection of mental health and identity, and how many folks within the Indigenous, Black, and communities of color still struggle with mental health.

Mental Health and the Global Majority

Tasha here. During the June 2020 demonstrations that occurred in the wake of the murder of George Floyd, mental health was a consistent topic no matter where you went, but it was especially relevant for younger generations of minoritized experience. However, it's unfortunate that communities that most often need mental health services are usually the ones that individually and structurally lack access to them, for a variety reasons.

Those hit by structural racism, poverty, and negligence usually don't have access to the resources needed to heal from personal and collective trauma. Let's dive into some barriers preventing access to mental health services for these communities.

1. **Lack of diversity/language barriers:** Most mental health providers are white. If a person of the global majority wants a provider who comes from—and can understand and empathize with—their background or might share some personal experience, they'll most likely come up empty. This lack of diversity creates painful gaps in understanding between health-care providers and the folks seeking treatment. Without truly understanding lived experiences or systematic injustices at work, providers might underestimate the effects of racism and discrimination on their patients, which could lead to weakened quality of care and support.

2. **Lack of financial accessibility/health care:** The United States doesn't have universal health care. The lack of financial accessibility in our health-care system often means that those most in need— those most vulnerable and minoritized—can't afford necessary health services.

3. **Cultural stigma:** This is a big one that hits home for me. Some families of the global majority hold cultural stigma around mental illness, and about seeking support in general. Strides have been made within the last decade to destigmatize mental health and therapeutic modalities for people of the global majority, but there's still a lot that needs to be tackled. While I can't and won't presume to generalize why many Black, Indigenous, and communities of color hold stigma about mental illness, I can speak to my specific experience. Many of my family members are immigrants. What I've realized over time is that much of their immigrant identity is centered on the ideals of self-sufficiency, perseverance, and resilience. Seeking help and support for anything that isn't physically debilitating is frequently perceived as weakness, a personal failing, or generally melodramatic. Growing up, I often heard that if someone was

dealing with something on a mental or emotional level, they just needed to "get over it" and move on. There are also layers of toxic masculinity and machismo that compound this way of thinking. All of this adds further shame and alienation to someone who's struggling. When we reduce mental illness to someone's being "too sensitive," we fail to recognize when things are serious. When I began my long, trying mental health journey, I felt conflicted discussing it with some members of my family—but I knew I needed and deserved support. After a lot of work, time, and understanding, we've come to a place where we can have conversations about my mental health if I choose to bring it up. This same struggle, however, is still present for many others.

Everyone deserves proper mental health support, especially those with minoritized experiences. Racism and systemic oppression are traumatic. Communities of the global majority have experienced collective trauma, which creates intergenerational trauma that affects future generations. In order for children to be able to reach their full potential, we must be willing to seek mental health services for them and for us without shame, we must have financial access to those services, and we must have diverse, inclusive representation among providers.

—Tasha

Make a Plan

It's taken a long time to put this one into practice. I've struggled to tease through what self-care meant for me. Before becoming antiracist, my self-care plan was a perfectly created Pinterest board full of self-soothing: bubble baths, wine, Netflix, and chocolate. It consisted of spending money to numb the heaviness of the world. Modern ideas of self-care have evolved under capitalist mechanisms to equate purchasing with self-soothing, usually targeted specifically to women buyers. Self-soothing colludes with white domination and capitalism for toxic positivity, silence, complacency, and avoidance.

This isn't to say that caring for the self is only ever defined as self-indulgence; self-care can be an act of nourishment, self-preservation, and resistance. During the highly intense 2020 presidential election, my self-care plan was a balance of effort and ease that allowed me to stay engaged. I'm aware I had immunity from exposure to the election. I'm a natural-born US citizen: if I wanted to, I could easily choose to disengage from US politics and voting. However, I knew that that was irresponsible. So, with this in mind, I was able to create a self-care plan that allowed me to *stay engaged* while staying balanced during the week of elections:

1. Turn off all news notifications and set calendar reminders to check my preferred news sources.
2. Start the day working out.
3. Take my time in the bathroom.
4. Grab coffee from my favorite local spot.
5. Clean our home with the children.
6. Play Uno or Trouble when I feel worried or anxious.
7. Make our favorite meal that always has enough leftovers.
8. Grocery shop for necessities.
9. Set a time to discuss the events (dinnertime).
10. If the forty-fifth president is reelected, forgive myself for not doing enough to change the outcome.

As a compassionate reminder, it's important to know where you are in the conversation in relation to your social identities. In other words, you should be aware of your immunities and marginalization. Again, it will inform you of your next steps. We'll always work to center the most marginalized, and that might include yourself.

Rethinking Self-Care

For parents and caregivers

Below are questions to answer with your family while you're cooking, waiting, driving, or walking together. I recommend the adults read and sit with these questions first, then integrate them into conversations with their children.

Questions to Consider:

- What's one habit you've created that serves you well?
- What are three little things you want to celebrate about yourself?
- What's the last thing you made that brought you joy?
- What's one thing you're thinking about but not quite ready to discuss with anyone? Do you think you're prepared to write it down or say it out loud to yourself?
- Let's daydream about possibilities together.
- What's something you're willing to give up so someone else can enjoy it?
- What do you need right now, this week, or this year to be your best self?
- What person deserves thanks for showing up for you (and it could be you)?
- What's one habit you want to unlearn?
- What's something you keep telling yourself that isn't true?

I dearly miss our neighborhood's daily modeling of community care.

Caring for Our Neighbors

Taking care of one another, or collective care as some call it, isn't the same thing as being nice. Yes, it's nice to wave, hold the door open for someone, say please and thank you, smile at the neighbor, etc. Those are all great manners to have, but they do not move the needle when it comes to justice work. Taking care of our neighbors is a constant act, rooted in fairness and community, and it happens on both an interpersonal level and a systemic level.

On a systemic level, we should notice ways our antiracist work can be embedded in our everyday lifestyle. Our younger ones can watch and remind us to pick up peanut butter, tuna fish, and fresh produce for our local food distribution sites. They can help us pack care packages for people without places to live, filled with first-aid kits, socks, water bottles, snacks, and gas station gift cards to pass out. They can go with us to vote, and understand how our voting will impact our neighbors. Our antiracist work means supporting public education, the public library, and public assistance. It means constantly considering who society works to make invisible and committing to supporting them.

On an interpersonal level, it's directly supporting the people we're in community with. When Hurricane Harvey struck Houston, our family experienced the widespread outpouring of community care. People waited hours just to sign up to volunteer and donated clothing, food, and materials to rebuild. I posted on Facebook that I was available to stop by and pick up items from people who wanted to donate, but didn't have use of a vehicle. Thanks to collective care, my children were soon in the backseat of our car, supplies stacked all around them, while I drove to neighbors' houses picking up donations to drop off.

Then a few educator friends and I organized a Kid-2-Kid service project. We rejected any notion of perfectionism and threw together a Facebook event. Families and friends shared it among neighbors, Girl Scout troops, cheerleading squads, and school circles. In just three days, the children created a project to pack gift bags for children in emergency shelters from kids who were still safe at home. In one afternoon, preschool, elementary, and secondary school children ended up packing over 2,400 bags that we distributed around to greater Houston emergency shelters. It's incredible what children can do when empowered by the adults in their life.

This one-time work is wonderful, but I want to offer you another idea. As Carter began to earn money, we noticed how quickly he would spend it on clothing and gaming items. Even though we have modeled redistribution of funds, Carter certainly didn't feel like it applied to him. Over breakfast, we discussed what we noticed and asked him, "What values are you communicating with your spending habits? Whose land are you working on and benefiting from?"

From there we were able to create a system for Carter that would align with our family values, such as finding ways we can contribute and redistribute to our community. Our family is committed to redistribution as an act of solidarity, and it's not only about funds. Your family might have the resources to share a particular set of skills with your neighbors pro bono (free headshots or résumé editing for Black, Indigenous, and people of global majority) or volunteer time at an organization of your choice.

Caring for the Environment

A few years ago, our family chose to move into a historically Black neighborhood in Houston. We rented a home there for a couple of years before being pushed out by gentrification. It was one of the few times I've lived in a predominantly Black neighborhood, unlike my partner, who's always lived in such neighborhoods. There were things I noticed immediately as different and unfair: the nearest playground was always littered with trash, the basketball nets were falling apart, there were huge anthills surrounding the playground, there were large furniture dumps all around our neighborhood, and there was constant police surveillance that did more harm than good.

Our garbage pickup rarely ran on schedule, even though we paid our bill on time every month. I would have to call 311 to repeatedly report another week of no garbage pickup. As our garbage cans sat in the street, waiting, the wind or rodents would often throw the garbage around. To outsiders, it might look like we didn't care for our neighborhood, but in reality, the city didn't care for our neighborhood.

For our homeschool recess, we chose a playground, where the city consistently mowed the lawn, treated the grass for fire ants, and maintained perfect basketball nets, that was ten minutes away on the other side of the highway. With the children, I would ask, "What do you notice is different about the two playgrounds?" As young as five, my children could identify what I was noticing. It's imperative that we blame systems and not individuals—after all, these are systemic failings happening. The City of Houston is responsible for cutting and treating the grass, keeping up with the nets, and dumping the garbage cans.

I don't want my children to believe the myth that Black people and communities of color do not take care of their environment. On the contrary, despite the mistreatment by the city, we see people providing more care of our environment—building community gardens, hosting garage sales, recycling aluminum cans and glass bottles, and contributing less environmental pollution—than their white counterparts.

The three Cs exist both in our homes and in our communities. We start to build expectations that we all need self-care, that we must be willing to think about and help one another, and that our community is worthy to be taken care of by us. As a family, my partner and I slowly introduce these three golden rules. During family time, we ask, "How did you take care of yourself today? What's one thing you did to care for others? How did you take care of your environment?" When you see your child holding the door open for a neighbor or calling a friend who was absent from school today, you can respond with, "Thank you for taking care of others." When parenting partners are watching our children for us (whoot whoot!), my partner and I make sure they're aware of our language for consistency. "Dad, after Carter eats, please ask him to take care of the environment before going back to play." When our children ask for screen time, I ask if they've cared for themselves, others, and their environment first. If they'd like to hang out with friends, play with their toys, or go skating, the same questions apply.

Preparing Your Home

In this section, we'll break down steps you can take to foster an empathetic, curious environment for developmental play.

Choosing Toys

Raising antiracist children calls us to use our antiracist skills to choose toys, books, and media that will recenter people of the global majority and provide accurate representation. At home, families of the global majority can work to provide "mirrors" for our children. We're preparing a home where their racialized cultural and ethnic identities become a source of pride and also normalized.

In my home, we exclusively had Black-presenting toys until our children were about six years old. We looked for Lego people, action figures, cars, clothes, accessories, dramatic play costumes, and play food that would affirm our children's culture. This was one small way we resisted upholding whiteness in our home.

White parents: When picking new toys for your home environment, look for toys that represent real people, places, and things to practice the language of human diversity. Look specifically for different skin tones, eye colors, hair textures, and culturally relevant accessories. White children, as early as age three, have a preference for their own racial group, and exhibit racial pre-prejudice toward Black children and adults, and people of the global majority. This might be exhibited by showing fear or discomfort around people of the global majority, choosing white playmates, and showing some of the same prejudices that exist in the world. In contrast, Black children show no negative bias or favoritism. Someone might ask, "Britt, why do some white children have a preference?" The better question is why don't Black and brown children have a preference, and how can we re-create that outcome? Black and brown children are regularly exposed to the world of diversity and discrimination. Diversity is expected from the very beginning, and is therefore truly normalized. The activity "How Diverse Is Your Universe?" will give you some direction about your child's preparation and exposure. Using toys is one way to prepare your child for the world of diversity, to practice accurate language and to recenter people of the global majority.

Choosing Media

One of my biggest failures is allowing nostalgia or convenience to be an excuse for my children to watch particular movies or TV shows. Repeat after me: *Nostalgia and convenience will never be justifiable reasons to expose our children to stereotypes and invisibility.* Research shows that more inclusive representation is increasing, yet children's media in the United States still centers thin, white, middle-class people.

A recent study conducted by the International Central Institute for Youth and Educational Television examined North American children's (up to age twelve) television content, including 476 programs with 1,654 main characters, on channels such as Cartoon Network, Disney Channel, Disney Jr., Nick Jr., Nickelodeon, Sprout–Universal Kids, and PBS Kids.[8]

- 65 percent of characters were white, and female characters were more likely to be non-white or racially ambiguous than male characters. This is almost representative of the racial makeup of the

US, as about 60 percent of the population is white, non-Hispanic, and non-Latine/x (US Census Bureau).

- Only 38 percent of characters were women or girls, while almost 51 percent of the US population is female (US Census Bureau).
- Female characters were twice as likely to solve problems using magic, while males were more likely to solve problems using science, technology, engineering, and math (STEM) or their physicality.
- 50 percent of female characters were shown to be wearing revealing clothing and had other physical traits that symbolize "sexiness." This is twice the number of males that were sexualized.
- The majority of characters were thin, and more females than males were portrayed this way. Research shows that women are vulnerable to images of thinness in media and that exposure can be harmful.
- Only 1 percent of characters had any sign of physical disability or chronic disease, while 20 percent of the population lives with a disability.
- 2 percent of characters were portrayed as having lower socioeconomic status, when about 20 percent of children in the US live below the poverty line (NCCP).

You might be wondering what your family can do to be more conscious, critical, and challenging. For families with children ages three to six, make a family-approved watch list with preselected shows. A few of our favorites are *Molly of Denali*, *Motown Magic*, *Nina's World*, and *Rise Up, Sing Out*. For families with elementary-aged children, in addition to continuing with a family-approved list, I encourage you to co-view shows that tackle discrimination and othering together. I've invited my parenting partner Saira Siddiqui to share her co-viewing practice, Critical Review of Media. For families with adolescents, encourage your children to create their own guidelines for viewing particular shows. When our children have pushed back, we make it clear that we don't support shows that choose to center white people or portray certain people as stereotypes.

A Critical Review of Media

For families with children ages six to twelve years old

Cops and robbers. Cowboys and Indians. The popular culture that surrounds our children is full of problematic ideas of "good" and "evil."

As a teacher-turned-parent, I knew I wanted to teach my children to challenge the archetypes of good guys and bad guys often found in movies or popular literature. As a Muslim parent that knew how my own community was often vilified, the importance of this activity was even greater.

When my children were elementary age, I decided to do an activity that allowed them to take a deeper look at who the heroes and villains were in the media they consumed. We created a T-chart, and at the top of the chart we put the words **heroes** and **villains**. We went through all their favorite cartoons, movies, TV shows, and books and made a list of as many heroes and villains as we could think of. We then asked ourselves the following questions:

1. What do they look like?
2. What do they sound like?
3. Do they have an accent?
4. What does their hair look like?
5. What color is their hair?
6. Do they have a beard?
7. Where are they from?
8. Do they have a difference in their abilities?

When the list was done we discussed any patterns or commonalities we found. We talked about the impact that these patterns have on kids and adults. We talked about where these patterns might come from. We talked about what these patterns could lead to out in the real world.

Though we did this activity once when they were young, the impact and lessons learned still inform their thoughts today. They pay attention now to the stories they consume and who serves as a good guy and a bad guy. They pay attention to this false idea that good guys are wholly good and bad guys are wholly evil. They pay attention to how the media and popular culture portrays certain races, communities, and cultures, particularly non-white cultures from around the globe. They pay attention to *who* created the story, *who* created this pattern, and *who* wrote the roles. And, more important, they pay attention when there's a break from this pattern. They notice what happens when writers come from marginalized communities. They notice when a cartoon feels different. They understand that often cartoons that feel different to them are ones in which traditional character arcs are ignored.

I learned the impact that one lesson can have on shifting our children's perspective and changing their trajectory. This single lesson served as that shift for my children.

Follow-up resources for parenting partners: the documentary *Reel Bad Arabs.*

—Saira Siddiqui

Choosing Books

Cobe started to listen to the Harry Potter books with his older brother. One day, a character named Lee Jordan was being described as "a Black boy with black hair and dreadlocks." Cobe immediately said, "That's odd. Why would they say he's Black?"

I responded with curiosity, "Why do you think the author wrote it?" Cobe replied, "Lee Jordan must really be proud to be Black. Because Harry Potter didn't say he was Black."

I then asked, "Is Harry Potter Black?" Cobe smiled and said, "Yes, Mom!" By listening to the books, Cobe imagined Harry Potter as a Black boy; his imagination saw himself as Harry. That's because in our house, Black people are represented as the default racialized identity for the main character, the hero, the villain, and the friend.

As a home working to affirm our children's Black culture, we expected our children's books to have Black main characters, characters of color, and stories full of love and humor until they were six years old. It was imperative that our children know they come from a place of power and that they're powerful before introducing stories of oppression. The message I'm sending to my children is that our culture is valuable enough to be centered.

For Indigenous, Native American, Pacific Islander, Asian American, African American, and Central and South American communities, the media continues to erase history, stories, and experiences simply by not recording them. This invisibility distorts history and upholds white domination ideology. The absolute truth then becomes that only white, European experiences happened and are valued.

When our children reached school age and actively asked to read books outside of our expectations, more often than not, those stories uphold and center whiteness. Instead of giving in to the status quo or yelling a quick "no," with a "because I said so," we had a family conversation focused on system thinking and balance.

1. What are the main characters' racialized identities?
2. Why do you think the author chose to center whiteness?
3. Is this something we want to support?
4. How could we recenter or balance what we are reading?

Representation matters only if we make it matter. We do that by intentionally choosing media that's truly representative.

Practices

The following section contains activities for caregivers and children around the topics covered in this part of the book. We'll begin with processing practices for the parenting partners first.

Developing Your Antiracist Lens

For families with children ages six and older

Here are some questions you can ask children while consuming media, whether reading, watching TV, or watching movies (also be sure to answer these questions yourself!):

Notice
- What do you notice about the characters/people, time, or environment in this story/current event?
- Who is racially present? Who is racially missing?
- What do you notice that may be unfair, harmful, or hurtful to someone or a group?

Consider
- How could we check on the person being harmed in this story?
- Why did the problem or situation arise?
- Who is affected by this problem or situation? How?
- What can be done to solve/fix/address the problem or situation?
- Who has the agency to do it?
- What are all the actions that could be taken given your considerations?
- Who could be involved to help?

Agency
- What risks were taken?
- What would you do?
- What are ways you could support those who would need it?

Accountability
- How did the characters see the action through to completion?
- How long did it take? Is the work finished?
- How can you use your position to raise awareness about the problem/situation?
- How can you support ongoing efforts toward antiracism?

Reading Articles to Learn and Unlearn

For parents and caregivers

Reading articles is one of our favorite tools to unlearn misinformation. It allows us to process on our own time, practice using the author's language, and then share our newfound information. As with any information, be sure to check that your articles come from a reputable source and are fact-checked.

As you read the article:

1. Take note of the title to see if it was written to evoke emotion.
2. Search the author's name, and check out their profile picture, bio, and previously published articles. How is the author experienced in this subject matter?
3. As you read the article, read for what confirms your previous knowledge and what challenges your currently held knowledge.
4. By the end of the article, aim to answer the following questions:

   a. What was the injustice?
   b. Who or what group experienced the injustice?
   c. Who or what is causing the injustice?
   d. What actions were taken or could be taken to create a different outcome?

Once done, sit with these answers and notice whether you've learned anything new about yourself through the answering process. If you have a parenting partner, consult each other after answering these questions to see the ways in which you have similar thinking and ways in which you have different thinking.

Sharing with Your Partners

For parents, caregivers, and adolescents

I built my community of parenting partners by sharing on social media. I resisted the idea that I knew it all and instead aggressively sought information I hadn't learned yet from others.

I find the 3Fs method extremely helpful to vulnerably share my misunderstandings and open the door to have conversations with my community. I first learned this method from Crossroads Antiracism Organizing and Training. I write a quick summary of the article using the 3Fs and share the article link with them when looking to both educate and be educated.

1. I felt . . .
2. I found . . .
3. I feel . . .

Example: "You know, before reading this article, I FELT _____, but then I FOUND _____, so now I FEEL _____!"

Afterward, I stay engaged with my partners because we're becoming together. With your family, community, and/or parenting partners, try using the 3Fs to communicate and foster growth, vulnerability, and engagement.

Documenting Your Care

For families with children of all ages

As a family, keep a running list of ways you're practicing the golden rules until it becomes your family's culture. Make your list on sticky notes or chart paper, or type them into an online document. Here's our list from one week of keeping track.

Care for Self	Care for Others	Care for the Environment
I brushed my teeth	I helped cook and bake	I dusted and watered the plants
I took a bath	I held doors open	I bought in bulk
I did my schoolwork	I made a birthday card	I used public transportation
I entertained myself	I read with a loved one	I took shorter showers
I drank water	I bought extra groceries to donate	I thought twice before buying more
I washed my hands	I donated clothes and toys	I grabbed a reusable water bottle
I slept	I grabbed the first-aid kit	I turned off unnecessary lights and water
I said no	I wrote a letter	I composted
I went outside	I played with my brother	I planted vegetables
I made doctor's appointments	I honored someone's no	I used reusable bags
I listened to music/ danced	I took care of pets	I recycled
I hung out with friends	I shared something	I completed chores

Collective Action for White Families

For white families with children of all ages

- Reach out to your child's school leadership and inquire how the curriculum supports students developing a white antiracist identity.
- Connect with local antiracist white folx to expand your impact within your community.
- Develop and refine your family or community plan for antiracist action that includes children. Children love to be thought partners. Include them in research and information gathering around:

  - Learning new vocabulary to ensure we're always centering humanity.
  - Where to shop to redistribute funds to folx of the global majority.
  - Who to vote for in local elections, including school board members.
  - Which policies to urge your elected officials to advocate for.
  - Which racial justice organizations you could be supporting for disruptive action in your local community.

When you encounter another white adult who expresses racist language, *engage* with them, especially if it happens in front of children. There is no reason to coddle racism; what we tolerate our children will embrace.

—Kerry LiBrando

Curating an Antiracist Book Collection

For families with children of all ages

This practice happens in three parts, and grows with your children. Each part works to strengthen your child's antiracist skills by using books as tools. If you find troublesome books, don't be afraid to discard those perpetuating harmful stereotypes and invisibility. Books are more impactful than anyone can measure. We're striving for our readers to experience accurate narratives through positive storylines and through historical truths. Always start by researching the author. What's their background and qualification for writing this story?

Ages infant to five years old

For children up to five years old, books can play a huge role in positively exposing them to different cultures and ethnicities. Look for books that represent real people, in present-day times. Model searching for accurate labels to identify the food, clothing, adornments, places, and other cultural characteristics. As you read the books, describe the people using the skin-tone language from Part Two and also your newfound words. Most important, find books featuring Black, Indigenous, and people of the global majority's love, joy, and everyday struggles.

Ages six to nine years old

Build a collection of books that provide a balance of narratives and informational stories. Books will be a mirror for our children: it will affirm their stories, experiences, and identities. This is where they get to practice their affirming language. Our book collection will also be a window: it will show them multiple perspectives, different experiences, and diverse identities. Windows, mirrors, and sliding glass doors is a concept created by Rudine Sims Bishop that can be beneficial when choosing books, podcasts, audiobooks, and toys. Right around six years old, your child will begin to understand concepts of time like the past, present, and future. Now is the time to introduce stories of discrimination and oppression. I recommend reading these books together. Too often, stories of discrimination and oppression like those about Ruby Bridges or the bus boycott are placed in our children's book collection for them to read independently and try to make sense of the discrimination. Young children are not equipped with the skills to unpack these injustices.

Ages ten to thirteen years old

According to Christopher Myers, for our older readers, "these children are much more outward-looking. They see books less as mirrors and more as maps. They are indeed searching for their place in the world, but they are also deciding where they want to go. They create, through the stories they're given, an atlas of their world, of their relationships to others, of their possible destinations." Here are some guiding questions to explore with your children:

1. Discuss how the character's identity is changing.
2. Which parts of the character's identity are they confident about?
3. What are the two opposing groups the character is struggling with?
4. Who accepts the character for who they are?
5. How is the character changing themselves in order to be accepted by others?

Part Three started our journey in raising antiracist children to think critically, develop specific liberating language, and become more aware. The content in this section focused on using antiracist skills to help develop a practice of questioning, wondering, and reflecting with children. Antiracist education cannot solely change the way people think about themselves; we're working to build critical thinkers and emotional literacy to combat white domination and patriarchal values, such as perfectionism.

As you navigate space, language, interpersonal dynamics, and family values with your antiracist skills, you should constantly be re-centering people of the global majority, looking for discriminatory systems at play, and creating space for conversations to happen with your family.

conscious consumption

As mentioned in previous parts, antiracism work is more than just a singular action you do every once in a while; it's a series of actions that will create a lifestyle. That means that as antiracists, we must constantly think critically and consciously about what we spend our money on, what we choose to consume, and how and what we choose to learn. This part of the book aims to dive into these questions so you can learn more, as well as offer some activities and practices you can do with your child.

I've invited my friend and colleague Aja Barber to share how she is consciously unlearning rich-white-supremacy expectations and the practices she is putting into place in her own life to ensure collective care.

Raising the Next Generation of Conscious Citizens

As a sustainability consultant and writer, part of my process for building my current body of work involved tracing the roots of my consumption and unpacking it. I found that childhood wounds from being made fun of for not having the right items (or wearing hand-me-downs) turned me into an ultra fast-fashion consumer obsessed with having the newest and next thing. For so long, so much of my self-worth was internally tied to buying and procuring new clothes and other new-to-market items. It was endlessly unfulfilling and always left me searching for the next thing. I thought that maybe if I had the just "right" thing . . . perhaps I'd finally be the kind of person that would've been allowed to sit at the cool kids' lunch table.

These insecurities lead to societal problems galore. Do we actually want all this abundance of new clothing being offered from stores pushing us to buy more and more? Do we think certain clothes, items, and memberships will complete or fulfill us? The desire to consume seeps in at very youthful ages in our society because we see it amplified everywhere. It's not just the advertisements we see in magazines, TV and films, billboards, and social media: it's even in schools.

So how do we raise the next generation to be citizens rather than consumers? How do we raise the next generation to see that their value isn't connected to the stuff they have? I believe it starts in schools. When I was a kid, children were very much made fun of for not having the right clothes. I believe that still goes on; it just happens away from adult eyes. And if it's not the clothes, it's the backpack, or the cell phone model. It's when kids come back from winter break and insist on gloating about the bounty they collected over the holiday season to their peers. It's the hypernormalization of shopping for disposable goods in our society as a pastime instead of valuing the things that really matter: love, generosity, kindness, and caring for your fellow human.

The next generation needs to know that the climate emergency we're facing is connected to the ways we buy and consume. Fast fashion is a problem of epic proportions causing worker mistreatment and environmental degradation. The end of many of our garments' life cycles ends up as a mess in someone else's backyard, most likely in the global South. A T-shirt isn't just a T-shirt, it stands for thousands of gallons of water to harvest the cotton, farmers who aren't being paid fair wages, and countries exploited for their materials. When children truly understand the systems behind everything we buy and how it reaches our hands, as well as how buying more won't fulfill them or make them more accepted . . . we can perhaps raise more informed citizens instead of consumers.

—Aja Barber

Raising a Generation of Conscious Citizens

American white domination manifests itself in all facets of our society, from what we choose to take part in to what we choose to consume. That means white domination, discrimination, and sexism are intrinsically linked to not only our policies, education systems, and societal standards, but our capitalist foundations as well. What we consume impacts us and our children, so being conscious about consumption is imperative in order to raise the next generation of conscious citizens.

What Do We Mean by Conscious Shopping and Consumption?

Shopping is what we spend our money on, and consumption is what we "take in." Shopping can be viewed as consumption, and what we "consume" can lead to certain shopping inclinations and choices, too. In this section, both these terms will be present. At the end of the day, the goal is to notice and learn the ways in which white domination asserts itself within our consumer practices and how we can do our part to combat it.

Helpful Definitions

Below, I dive into just a few terms you can introduce to your children to get the conversation started.

Sustainable—When it comes to conscious consumption, we can view sustainability in terms of maintaining and continuing the growth, protection, and advocacy of ecological balance by avoiding the overuse or complete depletion of natural, nonrenewable resources. The products we're using will return to the earth, so will the product be helpful or harmful when it returns?

Ethical—Consumption and consumerism are political acts, not unlike voting. According to the *Encyclopedia Britannica*, **ethical consumerism** is the idea that purchasers "consume not only goods" but also implicitly support "the process used to produce them" with their purchase.[1] So, by choosing one product over another, consumers can condone or condemn certain environmental and labor practices in a product's manufacturing process. If you're conscious about where you spend your dollars, the financial effects of economic boycotting will create incentives for companies to make production practices that better conform to consumer values and standards. Examples of successful results from ethical consumer movements are foods free of genetically modified organisms (GMOs), sweatshop-free clothing, and cruelty-free makeup.

Greenwashing—Greenwashing is a form of marketing spin in which a company's PR and marketing efforts deceptively convey a false impression of sustainability or environmentalism, or provide misleading information generally about how environmentally sound their products are. These types of marketing gymnastics are done to deceive consumers into believing that these products are environmentally friendly when they may not be. But don't be deterred: websites like Good On You,[2] the Slow Factory Foundation,[3] and Intersectional

Environmentalists[4] are here to help us. Check them out when you have the time to learn more. (Tasha here! I'd like to also include **rainbow washing**. This type of marketing gymnastics occurs every Pride month when corporations unveil new rainbow promotions, decorations, and products for their brand. Twitter photo backgrounds will be changed; employees from these companies might even march in your local Pride Parade. This charade of allyship, however, doesn't stop the fact that many of these same corporations and businesses donate money to politicians who endorse and create anti-queer and anti-trans legislation. The moral here: Always research who you're giving your money to. Don't be fooled by marketing!)

Fair trade—Fair trade is a pledge by a seller or company to provide fair wages and quality working conditions to those producing goods in poorer, exploited communities, in turn encouraging more equitable global trade. So if your child wants chocolate, you can purchase fair-trade chocolate with a certified fair-trade seal (this means a lot: in order to achieve that seal, producers and businesses must "adhere to strict labor, environmental, and ethics standards that prohibit slavery and child labor and ensure cocoa growers receive a steady income, regardless of volatile market prices").[5]

Renewable—Renewable resources are types of resources that can be found naturally and are abundant or can be replenished at the rate of usage in order to stay available. For example, we'll never run out of sun, so solar energy is a type of renewable resource, whereas coal and oil are not.

Setting Children Up for Success

We choose to support businesses led by Black, Indigenous, Latine/x, and Asian folks. We choose to support companies that are led by immigrants. We choose to support businesses that are led by folks of the

LGBTQ+ community. We choose to support disabled business owners. We choose to support women-led businesses.

We value inclusion. We embrace people. This includes the owners' and the employees' racial identity, gender identity and expression, physical abilities and disabilities, sexual orientation, income status, home language, and worldview.

On one shopping trip during the height of the COVID-19 pandemic, Cobe and I decided to venture inside a large chain store for some household necessities. It was November, which meant the store looked like a bad Christmas movie. But that didn't bother me; I looked at all the Christmas decor, imagining the golden acorns on my table and garlands on our spiral staircase. Usually, Cobe tries to get me out of the store, but this day he enjoyed looking at the decor, too. When Cobe turned to ask for a snow globe, it caught me by surprise. Nine times out of ten, our children are pretty good about upholding our expectation to not ask for extraneous things while shopping (we always go into a store with an understanding of getting only what we originally came for). I immediately wanted to say no: (1) we didn't discuss it when making a list, and (2) it didn't align with or uphold our spending values.

But I realized I hadn't had explicit conversations about conscious shopping and consumption with Cobe; I had not conveyed those spending values yet. At that moment, I asked him, "Is this by a Black-owned business?" I waited for his reply. When he didn't respond, I asked, "Is this a local store?" Again, I waited, because I wanted to invite Cobe into a conversation with me. Raising antiracist children is about creating the space for them to think and choose values. Then it becomes about commitments to the values by practicing them. In this moment, I was giving space to Cobe to think and choose his values and alignment.

When Cobe asked why those things were so important, I shared the crises Black-owned businesses were experiencing during the pandemic. According to *Forbes*,[6] Black-owned businesses experienced the most acute decline during COVID-19, with a 41 percent drop. Businesses with Latine/x owners fell by 32 percent, and Asian-owned businesses dropped by 26 percent. The decision to support businesses owned by people of the global majority was to recenter those most impacted by the pandemic. It was then that Cobe understood why I asked him those questions, and why I drew a hard line about the extraneous purchase.

There will be an activity at the end of this part dedicated to making a list of locally owned businesses for you and your children to use. Use that activity to start conversations about community conscientiousness and supporting your local economy.

Defining Our Understandings: Small, Local, and Family Businesses

I often ask my readers to support locally owned businesses and businesses of color. I don't make the disclaimer of "whenever you can," because truth be told, we all could support them a lot more than we do. One time, I was met with a paternalistic comment in response to this call to action: "What about the people who can't afford to shop at the small business? As much as I understand where you're coming from, I worry for those in low socioeconomic groups who might read a post like this and feel like shit." I thought this exchange would be a perfect time to unpack common misconceptions about small and local businesses.

Small businesses don't refer to a particular price point or brand identity, it's a political and economic distinction. Not all small businesses are created equal. I prefer to use the terms **local**, **family-owned**, or **neighborhood** when referring to my conscious shopping habits.

Back to the reader's comment: I don't know where this person got this idea, nor why they feel inclined to "worry" about poor folks in this way. Working-class and poor folks support local businesses all the time. Their local barbershop, hairstylist, nail technician, "the meat-man" and "candy-lady," their local corner store, their community-supported agriculture (CSA), the repair shop, the laundromat, and many of their neighborhood food spots are local businesses. While #shoppingsmall has the brand identity of overpriced, white-owned, bespoke businesses and boutiques, with zero-waste body washes and candle-making kits, it certainly doesn't represent all local or community businesses. Under-resourced communities are full of small businesses and their community members are already #shoppingsmall.

Choosing PoGM-Owned Businesses

Supporting Black, Indigenous, and people of the global majority–owned businesses is a necessary requirement for antiracism. It's a critical action we take to recenter businesses of the global majority by financially committing to communities who are directly experiencing racism and xenophobia. I draw on the work of Ida B. Wells, a journalist, activist, and researcher, in the late nineteenth and early twentieth centuries. Ida B. Wells became one of the first investigative reporters on the scenes of lynchings. As she researched and interviewed people, she noted the stereotype of Black men raping white women was usually a cover for what was really white backlash to Black men growing economically independent.

In 2021, we marked the one-hundred-year anniversary of the 1921 Tulsa Race Massacre. According to Aaron Morrison from the Associated Press: "The Tulsa Race Massacre is just one of the starkest examples of how Black wealth has been sapped, again and again, by racism and racist violence—forcing generation after generation to start from scratch while shouldering the burdens of being Black in America."[7]

Every major Black leader has called on us to divest from large corporations and invest in Black-owned businesses. Supporting Black- and Indigenous-owned businesses means investing in communities. It's not only an economic act, it's a political and social act for change. Luckily, there are several databases and even apps around today to help us locate and shop at Black, Indigenous, and people of the global majority businesses. At the end of this part, there will be a few activities dedicated to scoping out and supporting the Black, Indigenous, and Asian American and Pacific Islander–owned businesses in your neighborhood.

Our Family's Approach to Supporting Small Businesses

Supporting local businesses requires patience and humility. The customer experience might not be as well executed as one would like; it might not have curbside pickup, online ordering, or a drive-thru or offer free samples, and that's okay. I've learned that I have had to check my expectations and take note of what they do offer instead. They might have a friend or neighbor working that day, a donation tin available for a community organization, fliers inviting you to the next city council meeting, and local business cards and posters on display. As Saira Siddiqui says: "Small businesses and neighborhood businesses don't receive the money breaks and opportunities afforded to largely white, largely corporate-owned businesses. It's important to be mindful of the fact that sometimes, these places might not be as pristine as your local corporate franchise." The question is always why. Small businesses struggle to secure business loans, which limits their cash reserves to make costly additions and upgrades. Small businesses also don't have the personnel departments corporations lean on for marketing and advertising, innovation, and customer service.

Using our antiracist skills, we can (and should) investigate the unique intersection of challenges and obstacles locally owned businesses that are also Black- or Indigenous-owned face in order to best support them and their success.

Make a firm rule that lasts all year about where and how you'll spend your dollars. Every family's rule will be different because of income, resources, geographical location, and access. The important part is to communicate the intention with your children. For us, we purchase necessities (toilet paper, paper towels, soap, detergent, etc.) from big-box stores. We split our grocery shopping between our "homegrown" grocery store and a chain. We purchase our wants from local, family, and neighborhood businesses and creators.

This also means that we don't expect small businesses to . . .

- Have round-the-clock business hours
- Have large quantities of a product
- Offer free shipping
- Give massive markdowns/sales

Instead, we . . .

- Honor the business days and times posted
- Join their waiting list/mailing list for the next release
- Accept that shipping is our responsibility
- Trust the price they're charging

Small businesses are not monolithic, and it's not our intention to paint them with a broad stroke—it's our intention to expand our idea of small business so we can become conscious citizens.

The Credit Card Game

Large airline industries, major hotel chains, rental car companies, large chain stores, and ride-sharing companies all work together to keep your money circulating with them and only them, effectively shutting out local and smaller businesses. When we choose to ring everything up on our credit cards and spend money at their chosen companies for double points, cash back, and low-financing options to vacation south of the border on stolen and colonized land, we take money away from our neighborhood businesses and funnel it into major conglomerates instead. If you like the perks but don't want to perpetuate the problem, look into credit cards that offer points and cash back on all purchases, not just designated ones. Or agree to use the credit card for fixed bills while using cash and debit cards with your family-owned businesses.

Shopping with Values

As stated in Part One, our values for our children to become conscious citizens are rooted in: **authenticity**, **curiosity**, **collaboration**, **accountability**, **becoming**, **empowerment**, and **candor**. These values directly disrupt corrupting actions, support critical thinking, and allow our children to live out values of justice. In this section of shopping and consumption, we work to be curious about the production pipeline, the employee benefits, and the sustainability plans. We acknowledge that we won't be perfect with our actions, and we won't always have the resources to shop and support the businesses we want. However, we are honest about what we're doing, what we can do better, and what we will stop doing in the name of justice.

Know Before You Go: The History of Minimum Wage

Since the late 1930s, the US government has held firm to the belief that all workers are entitled to a base hourly pay. Which workers receive that minimum—and how much that minimum is—has unfortunately been a political issue since the idea was introduced. The reason for this friction is that the federal minimum wage doesn't automatically take into account (and therefore adjust to) the rising cost of living, so since the late 1960s, the minimum wage lagged behind inflation considerably. By 2019, only eight states made the move to automatically increase their minimum wages based on the cost of living.[8]

Supporting a Living Wage (and Why It Matters)

It's unfortunate that raising the minimum wage continues to be a political issue when people are working forty hours a week but can barely afford to make rent. The minimum wage is simply the minimum amount an employer can legally pay their employee. The minimum wage is supposed to (barely) keep people out of poverty. A *living* wage would mean people would be above the poverty level. With this in mind, look into the places you frequent to notice whether they support their employees with a minimum wage that's adjusted to the local cost of living. You can model these ethics to your child by inquiring about a business's pay to their employees together and creating shared family values to frequent only the businesses that do so. From the cashier that checks you out at the grocery store to the waiter who takes your brunch order, these folks are members of your community and are a part of your daily lives. With gentrification occurring every day, raising the cost of living and pushing people of the global majority out of their own neighborhoods, ensuring you support businesses that value and respect their employees is imperative.

Say No to Cultural Appropriation

As mentioned in Part One, cultural appropriation happens when we take pieces or practices of a minoritized culture and use them out of context, change the meaning, diminish the significance altogether, and/or sell them for profit. This happens all the time with clothing and hair: many companies, influencers, and celebrities will dabble in trying out (and usually profiting from) the aesthetics of different cultures. Black women can get penalized for wearing braids or cornrows at work, oftentimes being labeled unprofessional or unkempt, but when white celebrities do it, it creates a new, cool "trend" magazines rave about.

Another instance is when clothing companies sell traditional clothing with a Western spin for a white audience. This leads to white teens wearing the traditional Chinese garment *qipao* to prom, or clothing companies crafting loose-fitting "kimono" cardigans and shawls modeled by white women on their website. Both the garments used as examples here—the *qipao* and the kimono—are traditionally worn for important celebrations, sacred ceremonies, and notable milestones. Divorcing them from their cultural context through monopolization, misunderstanding and disregarding their importance, and selling them for profit is culturally offensive and unethical. Taking these treasured, culturally significant staples and subjecting them to American consumerism in order to cater to an uninformed white audience is just the latest manifestation of colonialism and imperialism. We can teach children to be more culturally caring and aware, and more conscious of which businesses they support. Never be afraid to call out cultural appropriation, and never be afraid to have discussions about it with your children. I've invited my parenting partner Joemy Ito-Gates to share more about cultural appropriation and how to combat it below.

Cultural Appropriation: My Kimono Is Not Your Costume

Kimono is sacred. We wear them for important ceremonies, rituals, and festivals both in Japan and globally as part of the Japanese diaspora. They're often handed down in families and carefully stored away for important occasions. For families that had their kimono and traditional garments destroyed, left behind, or stolen because of the incarceration of Japanese heritage people in North America and Latin America during World War II, the absence of kimono is tied to a larger story of intergenerational trauma that's compounded by the absence of this history being present in our school's textbooks and curriculums.

In my own multiracial family that's Black, Filipino, Japanese, and white, teaching our child to value and honor her rich heritages is extremely important to us. Part of how we nurture our child's connection to her ancestors and family stories is through our cultural garments. We know that we cannot rely on the mainstream education system to teach our child about cultural pride and history, so it's up to us as her parents to provide her with those opportunities. After my child turned three years old, we took her to the Buddhist Temple in San Francisco for her Shichi-Go-San Ceremony. It's a Buddhist ceremony that's meant to confer blessings on children who reach the ages of three, five, and seven, so that they may live long and abundant lives. I dressed in one of my grandmother's kimono with red maple leaves for the fall season and my child wore her first kimono that day; her excitement and pride was palpable. She was beaming and understood that we wear kimono to honor our culture, our ancestors, and ourselves. We took professional photos that day and it's my child's favorite photo of herself because she remembers the joy of wearing kimono with Mama.

When I see garments called "kimono" that are not in fact kimono, or kimono being worn as a costume, or Japanese traditional clothing being commodified in any number of ways by people who have racial power, it hurts and feels like my community is getting erased: our voices, our stories, and our diaspora histories.

In 2020, we saw an exponential rise in Anti-Asian violence that's tied to a legacy of silencing and erasing Asian heritage people. This ongoing violence is part of the web of white supremacy. Even though I have been gaslit, harassed, and trolled for being outspoken against the cultural appropriation of kimono and Japanese cultural garments in fashion and sewing communities, which is its own kind of anti-Asian hate, I know that working against cultural appropriation is part of cutting the threads of the web of white supremacy. Eventually it will weaken and can be replaced with more liberatory and inclusive practices: practices where our voices are heard and valued, our stories are uplifted and cherished, and our histories are taught and remembered, every day, every month, always.

—Joemy Ito-Gates

How Does the Patriarchy Promote Gender Consumption and White Domination?

The patriarchy and racism work hand in hand to place fairer-skinned (white) women above dark-skinned women in terms of beauty, value, and safety. It also works to ensure people have a reliance on products that claim to help them get closer to Eurocentric and patriarchal standards of beauty. These products could be from as normal as makeup to as sinister as skin-bleaching cream.

This isn't to say that anyone who enjoys wearing makeup is subscribing to this ideology: makeup can be a wonderful way for people to find joy and self-expression! It also can be an important cultural touchstone for many communities. What this section is critiquing specifically is the way society pressures people, especially women and girls, to look and act a certain way. As long as shame or racism aren't the basis for the purchases, we can feel comfortable indulging in our beauty exploration. By checking in with ourselves and investigating the desire to adhere to beauty trends that align us with white supremacist ideals of beauty, we can hopefully be a guiding light for our children to show that their own skin and their own features are beautiful, no matter what societal Eurocentric standards claim. I've created space for my parenting partner Trisha Moquino to share more about makeup, culture, and profits.

Who's Profiting?

Trisha Moquino is raising her sixteen-year-old and thirteen-year-old in her hometown of Cochiti, Kewa, and also in Ohkay Owingeh, in New Mexico. She and her husband are raising their two teenage daughters to be connected to their Keres language and cultural ways of being. She aims for her children to feel good about who they are in their own skin without American capitalism demanding they need particular products to be or look beautiful. She is an elementary teacher, school administrator, organizer, and board member working to center contemporary Indigenous history in schools today.

When I chat with my friend Trisha Moquino, we often discuss the challenges we share in raising teenagers. We both hope our teenagers will (1) feel comfortable and confident for who they already are and for who they're becoming, (2) think good things about themselves even when it's difficult, and (3) be proud of themselves and their family.

"You don't need to wear makeup to be beautiful. Our grandparents taught us not to rush into wearing makeup. They stated that our creator made me the way I was supposed to be and that I was fine that way, I was beautiful that way." Trisha continues to share these teachings with her daughters to emphasize to them their cultural beliefs and values.

Trisha has offered a few questions she asks her daughters when they're discussing makeup, some about beauty standards, some about white supremacy and capitalism's role in the desire to adhere to them; you'll find them in the practice section. It's important to note, this isn't a new conversation for Trisha's family; they've been talking about self-love with her girls for a long time.

There are numerous products on the market ready to take our money to fix that, tone this, or eliminate something. These products send a powerful message to our children that there's a "right" kind of body, and if you don't have it, don't worry: you can purchase the products to fix yourself to get closer to that more "acceptable" body type. While we challenge this lie, we want our children to know that our bodies will grow, stretch, and age with time.

It's our goal for children to understand why companies are pushing highly photoshopped pictures and have narrow casting calls to sell their products.

1. Review social media ads and newspaper fliers with your children. Ask your child to think about the messaging: "What's the company saying is the problem and the solution?"

2. Compare Photoshop-free ads (from brands that have pledged not to use Photoshop in their advertisements) and photoshopped ads to open a conversation about body diversity and natural development. Discuss how cellulite, stretch marks, body hair, and acne are all normal changes that happen to growing bodies.

3. Explicitly call out bogus products that mislead consumers. Talk with your children about how the product doesn't match the messaging and how that's false and unfair. Together, write letters to the companies demanding accurate and truthful advertising.

4. Set a firm boundary; no one should be shamed about their growing body or feel embarrassed about their body. **Body-shaming** is making fun of someone's body, size, or shape with critical comments. Work hard to make your family a body-shaming-free zone. In our home, I've set the expectations that other people's bodies are not available for critiques or comments, and in turn, no one should critique or comment on our bodies. This also means I do not share negative comments about my body, either.

Discussing Makeup with Children

For families for children of all ages

Self-expression is vital and should be encouraged, and makeup can be a great tool to explore identity, beauty, and expression. As parents and caregivers, it's important, however, to encourage children to reflect on their curiosity about dabbling with makeup to investigate where their interest stems from.

When approaching this subject with my children who've voiced the desire to buy and wear makeup, I ask them the following questions:

1. Why do you want to wear makeup? (This is important because we want to investigate if this is a desire to experiment with self-expression, or for another reason, such as shame or pressure to adhere to Eurocentric beauty standards.)
2. How much will this cost you? Financially and emotionally?
3. How will you feel if you wear makeup?
4. Who financially profits from you wearing makeup, and/or who will not profit off of you if you choose to not wear makeup?
5. How can you make sure you choose products that will be safe for your skin?
6. How can not wearing makeup be good for the earth? (This is also an opportunity to delve into ethical processing/manufacturing practices.)

Have these conversations with an open mind with your child, and encourage them to think critically about their desires, instincts, and thoughts about these potential purchases.

—Trisha Moquino

Analyzing the Pink Tax

For families with children ages ten and older

About half of the US population is subject to the **pink tax**, which is the occurrence of higher-priced items marketed toward women (usually in pink packaging), such as hygiene items, women's razors, and women's body wash. Logistically, there's no real difference between many disposable drugstore razors marketed to either men or women except the packaging, yet many women's razors are marked up at a much higher price than men's razors. It's the same with body wash; there's no large difference between the standard ones marketed to men and women, and yet women often pay far more for these products. In addition to reinforcing gender binaries, this insidious practice can cause individuals who select these pink-packaged products to pay hundreds of dollars more per year. When we remember that women are usually paid less than men for the same job, the economic disparity becomes worse.

As an exercise, take your child to your local grocery or drugstore and examine the differently marketed products for men and women.

1. Select two products by the same brand that are marketed to two different genders. Review the prices to note whether the one marketed toward women costs more than the one marketed toward men.

2. Help your child compare the components of the products: aside from scent and color, is there a notable difference in ingredients and formulations for the gendered body wash, shampoo, or antiperspirants? Many of these products actually have the same ingredients, manufacturers, and ratings/recommendations.

3. Encourage them to think critically and analyze the information they're viewing. If there's indeed a disparity between prices but not a disparity between ingredients or components, ask your child about whether or not this difference in price is fair.

The Invisible Labor We Demand

In this section, I'll break down emotional labor and intellectual labor, how they relate to each other, and how they connect to consumption, capitalism, and discrimination.

While writing this book, I unlearned and relearned the meaning of emotional labor. I thought emotional labor was about the energy it took to educate another person about their racist actions and beliefs. I had reduced emotional labor to an individual act between myself and someone I had a relationship with: my dad, my sister, or my beloved. But after reading a *Vogue* article titled "'Emotional Labor' Is Not What You Think It Is," I learned that the phrase was actually coined by sociologist Arlie Hochschild in her 1983 book *The Managed Heart: Commercialization of Human Feeling*, and refers to "a situation where the way a person manages his or her emotions is regulated by a work-related entity to shape the state of mind of another individual, such as a customer."[9]

We have to discuss emotional labor in the context of power and profit. We've all heard the phrase "the customer is always right." Emotional labor is about the numerous times a person is wrong, hurtful, and committing microaggressions, yet the victim is expected to be silent with a smile. Emotional labor requires someone to suppress or devalue their own emotions and reactions to avoid rocking the boat and upsetting someone else. People of the global majority in service roles in particular are expected to stomach and tolerate microaggressions and racist and harmful language with zero support from their employers. They're forced to prioritize the customer experience over their own humanity if they want to keep their job. The expectation is for them to care more about the company's bottom line than themselves. Now I understand: **emotional labor** is much more than a friend assuming I have the capacity to engage or assuming my choice to educate them; the term has evolved to include these things, but the origin of the term is about a power dynamic of who's allowed to own their feelings when profits and systems of power are involved.

This newfound definition reminds me of an experience Katie shared with me. They were traveling back from a work trip and waiting for their flight to board. While sitting at the gate, they overheard someone's voice getting louder and louder. They noticed a white woman demanding an upgraded seat for the flight at the check-in counter. The airline customer service agent, a Black man, continued to deny her request. As her entitlement grew, so did her voice. Finally, she demanded to know his name, the name of his supervisor, and the supervisor's phone number to "get him fired." Without skipping a beat, Katie walked over, talked to the check-in officer, and asked for the same information. While the woman was still standing there, Katie loudly said, "I want to let your supervisor know how well you're handling this unfortunate situation, and that this customer is way out of line with you."

This kind of emotional labor and abuse happens often. A customer doesn't get their way and then complains to management. With social media, incidents like this are being documented often. Katie models for us one way we could handle this situation if we're ever witnessing it.

On a more personal level, requests for free time, education, and "pick-my-brain coffee dates" can be described as **intellectual labor**. Minoritized people have often been thrust into the educator role on topics of antiracism, sexism, ableism, transphobia, homophobia, and more, without ever having sought that responsibility in the first place. While some are fine being placed into this educator role, many are placed there by default. Usually, this entails people of the global majority providing information and being available for not only questions, but even *debates* on the validity, pain, and history of their experiences, just so white people can "better understand."

Below are a few suggestions to expand your knowledge and

understanding about the experiences of others, and doing these steps with your children will give them strategies to educate themselves:

1. **Google it**—Before asking a person of the lived experience to teach you the basics, google your question. There are plenty of articles, books, videos, and documentaries on the history, lived experiences, and struggles of a variety of different identity groups, both free and available for purchase. Take the step to educate yourself first before asking someone to explain what's available to you elsewhere.

2. **Pay for their time**—If someone takes the time to educate you and patiently hear your many questions, pay them. Even if they freely offer to provide you the information, show that you value their time and consideration. If someone is going out of their way to inform you, show gratitude and grace by sending them money, or even offering to buy them dinner or a coffee. Keep in mind you're most likely not the only person they've done this for. Lastly, remember that there are people who do antiracism education as their job—take their workshops and spare your friends the impromptu tutoring session.

3. **Be mindful of *what* and *how* you're asking**—Inviting a person of a minoritized identity to share their experience and feel seen and heard is one thing, but asking them to relive pain, microaggressions, and/or delve into personal details can be retraumatizing for them, especially if the space is not safe. Oftentimes college admissions essays fall into this trap: many prompts will ask students to write about the "challenges" they've had to overcome, usually in a small enough word-count restriction that limits the possibility for nuance. While some students' challenges might solely be academic, many students of the GM have had different challenges to overcome. This isn't to say that adversity and resilience aren't worthwhile and shouldn't be celebrated, but people of the global majority often feel reduced to these experiences and these experiences only. Additionally, these college prompts often suggest that there should be an arc of having

conquered, overcome, and prevailed over these struggles, but this isn't always the case. People of the global majority live through discriminatory experiences every day, and sometimes, there is no conquering. Sometimes there's only surviving.

If you're mindful of what you're asking, when you're asking, and how you're asking for information and education, you'll model that same considerate behavior to your children, as well. Additionally, this section hopefully conveys how intellectual and emotional labor can be connected. These two asks aren't always mutually exclusive; they'll impact the individual on both fronts. We should raise our children to value the contributions, experiences, and intellectual labor of those around them, and these steps are a great place to start.

Lastly, know that you can acknowledge and value any and all intellectual labor contributions from people of the global majority, even if you've casually requested to "pick" someone's brain about something. All work is work; all efforts matter. Grab your colleague a coffee and say thank you.

Environmentalism, Consumption, and Your Family

Now that we've delved into terms and history, let's go into environmentalism, antiracism, and you. There's a lot here to honor, consider, and unlearn, but just like with other sections, educating yourself and laying the foundation for new habits and outlooks will be pivotal for your antiracist parenting journey. Don't forget to open yourself up to learning by dropping your defenses.

Intersection of Culture, Race, and Tradition

On November 25, 2019, Vice President Kamala Harris tweeted: "Who else keeps their spices in Taster's Choice jars? Turns out @Mindy

Kaling and I have more in common than we initially thought."[10] The Indian community came together on Twitter for a group-wide chuckle. When #growinguphispanic was trending on Twitter, several followers all laughed (and commiserated) about opening their *abuelas'* blue tins of butter cookies eager for a sweet snack, only to find sewing supplies.[11] While #decluttered and #organized homes have millions of followers who might think to purchase a set of forty-eight matching containers, we can simply reuse jars and cookie tins for a more sustainable action.

The neat thing about culture is that it can only be experienced. The way we choose to set up our kitchen—how we display the spices, what we leave on the counter, what we store in the pantry or on the floor—is all a part of our deep cultural practices. Environmentalism continues to erase Black and brown people from the sustainability conversation even though many sustainable actions are baked into our cultural practices.

The Three R's: An Intersection of Community and Location

When we think of the three R's (reduce, reuse, and recycle), perhaps we think of water bottles, Tupperware, and soda cans. But these R's can be applied outside of paper, plastic, and aluminum; we can think of them in terms of community care. Instead of relying on a big-name store to buy the latest products, we can make a day of thrift store shopping, garage sale browsing, and online community sales posts. We can keep these same considerations in mind when looking to re-home clothes, toys, or furniture. Dress for Success is just one example of a nonprofit organization with many locations that aims to help women achieve economic independence by providing professional attire in order to secure employment. Toys that our children no longer use would be treasured if you donated them to your local family or women's shelters, or even a local day care. All you'd need to do is get in touch with the director of those organizations and ask if/how you can donate. There are also several organizations and charities—such as your local Furniture Bank—that would gladly take furniture off your hands to provide it for direct reuse by local families who can't afford to furnish their homes. Thrift stores are great, but oftentimes extraneous items that don't get sold end up going into landfills anyway.

In your home, stash a milk crate or large container for your family to routinely put items you no longer need. Explain to your children that this is not a trash bin, it's a place for items we no longer need and will be useful to someone else:

1. "You don't seem to play with this doll anymore. Could we share it with a child who would want it?"
2. "Is there something you're not using anymore? Let's redistribute it!"
3. "Any clothes you've outgrown? Anything that doesn't fit? Let's share it with someone else."

You can make these donation trips with your children to teach them early on about giving back and about collective care.

I've invited my friend and literary auntie Christine Platt to share how she applies her less-is-liberation framework to help foster collective care.

Less Is Liberation for Adults *and* Children

For parents and caregivers

One of the greatest lessons we can teach children (and embrace ourselves) is being content with what we have. Whenever a parent or caregiver complains, "My child just has so many things!" I remind adults that they're the ones who are responsible for the excess. Adults are in control of what's allowed into and remains in the lives of young people in their care. Therefore, it's our responsibility to not only help children manage their current excess but also ensure that their lives are as simplified as possible going forward. Here are a few ways you can help young people embrace being content with only the things they need, use, and love:

Check Yourself

Often, adults contribute to children's excess because they're fulfilling their own unfilled childhood wants and desires. Reflect on how you were taught to manage money, how your family celebrated milestones and achievements, and consider whether growing up with scarcity or abundance may be influencing your spending, celebratory, and consumption habits.

Learn to Say, "No, Thank You."

Refusing to accept an item because it doesn't align with what you're teaching your children or will contribute to their overconsumption of toys and books isn't rude—it's setting boundaries. You can do this with family members, and even with birthday gifts, party favors, and other freebies. You must learn to not allow these items into your life out of obligation, and you should show your children you're committed to not having more than you need. You must remember, once you accept something into your child's life, they'll feel responsible for it and quickly form an attachment. This makes it even harder for your child to let go.

Get Creative

The best birthday party that my now adult daughter had (and the only one she remembers!) was when she celebrated her eighth birthday. Her room was already cluttered with more toys than she needed and so, in lieu of gifts, we asked guests to bring an item for our local food pantry. The children were totally into this idea. Every family gifted *bags* of groceries, and the kids still had an amazing time playing together. Use this example to get creative about party ideas and gift giving. These moments are amazing opportunities to teach your children that they have enough . . . and that they can still have fun while helping others.

Try a Different Approach

Scolding children about being messy or irresponsible with their belongings may not always yield the result you want. Instead, give them an opportunity to determine what they need, use, and love, and give them the opportunity to let go of what no longer serves them. Hand your child a donation bag and ask them to fill it with some of the toys, books, and clothing they no longer enjoy so they can help other children who are less fortunate. Don't be surprised if that bag is filled within the hour. They may even ask for another! Children are naturally compassionate, and so sometimes, it's all in the approach.

When children are able to manage their belongings, it's liberating for everyone!

—Christine Platt

Environmental Racism

Regarding what's traditionally associated with the three R's, we should have conversations early on with our children about the usage of resources and how we care for our planet. Plastic starts as a fossil fuel and is acquired through the process of fracking and transported through pipelines. Pipelines destroy much of the land they're built on, and usually they go through under-resourced communities or communities of color. These pipelines transport that fuel to oil facilities, eventually transforming it into plastic resin. As the Climate Reality Project describes, local residents exposed to the toxins released near these oil facilities can have higher chances of cancer, cardiovascular and respiratory disease, and childhood leukemia,[12] and there are several studies that show these sites disproportionately impact communities of color.[13]

When it comes to plastic disposal, landfills and incineration sites are more often than not placed near under-resourced communities and communities of color: according to a 2019 report from the Global Alliance for Incinerator Alternatives (GAIA,) 40 percent of MSW incinerators currently operational in the US are "in communities where both the thresholds for poverty and the percentage of people of color" are above 25 percent. Forty-eight incinerators are in communities where "more than 25 percent of the population is below the federal poverty level" and forty-four are in communities where the population is at least "25% people of color."[14] Exploited communities are typically targeted with more plastic packaging and single-use products in their local markets that end up polluting their neighborhoods.[15] The impact of these disproportionate environmental hazards is known as **environmental racism**, and we can do our part by purchasing less plastic (and reusing/recycling what we can). On a system level, we can advocate for better policy health regulations and joining them in their community-led oppositions to these sites being put up. Join and support communities of color on their mission to hold these industries accountable for their environmental and health impacts. If we communicate the ideal of collective care and collective responsibility early on, we can teach our children that public health is important, and that we must always protect and advocate for vulnerable, minoritized communities.

Getting Started

When you choose to spend money on something, you're providing money to that company or person so they can continue their production the way they've done it. As mentioned, remind children that items aren't made in a vacuum; they're made by companies and people, and they're made in a certain way.

Needs versus Wants

Around six years old, children are ready to begin conversations about "needs versus wants." Our family leans on the work of Dr. Maria Montessori to help define our common need: the desire to live. The desire to live creates in all human beings both spiritual and physical needs. Physical needs consist of clothing, nourishment, transportation, communication, shelter, health, and defense/safety. Spiritual needs are religion and philosophy, cultural markers, and social acceptance. Each of these are represented in every human civilization past and present but look different, depending on the climate of the region and its people's skills, technology, and beliefs. For children six to nine years old, we'll work to build awareness about our needs. This is important for two reasons: First, we want children to understand when they're asking for a need or a want. Second, we want children to grow up and advocate for the needs of others. For example, our children know all humans need shelter to secure our possessions and to keep us safe from dangerous weather and other pernicious elements. We connect this to our voting practices: we'll vote yes to increase access to affordable housing and increase wages because everyone needs a safe place to live.

Needs versus Wants

For families with children ages six to nine years old

Here are some examples of how you can begin talking to your six- to nine-year-olds about needs versus wants:

1. First, ask your child, "Can you name any needs?" Children at this age typically have this word in their vocabulary, so they should be able to answer this. What I found from personal experience was that about half of my children's responses were needs, and half were wants.

2. Next, ask your child, "Can you name any wants?" Once again, I found that about half of their responses were wants and half were needs.

3. Then, define the two: "A need is something we *can't* live without; it's something all humans require. A want is something we *could* live without. It might be a preference or something very individual; for example, I have a preference to have a pool, I have a preference to have a bathtub, I have a preference for using a car (not going on the subway)."

4. Do some crafts together! We got an 11"×19" poster board that we drew a T-chart on. We titled it *Needs and Wants*. I encouraged the boys to go through magazines and cut out images to then paste under either the need or the want section. You can encourage your family to draw or write in the spaces instead. Discuss how to think critically about why something is in one section versus the other.

5. Afterward, notice what your children might have left off of their needs list. For example, both of my children left medicine off of their needs list. With this in mind, I made a note to myself to have a conversation with them next time we went to the drugstore about how health care and medicine are needs and rights that everyone should have access to.

6. When children are nine years old, they can do research projects on fundamental needs in different civilizations and the history of access to those needs. What was ancient Rome's transportation system like? What were the clothes like in ancient Egypt? What was the agricultural system like for your local Indigenous tribe pre-colonization? How did the climate and natural resources affect the needs of those civilizations? What were the wants like? What were the wants that the wealthy and royalty gave themselves?

Antiracist Grocery Shopping Practices

Food equity is a systemic issue to be solved on political, economic, social, and individual levels. Access to healthy food creates social, emotional, cognitive, and physical benefits for people, and right now structural racism is affecting those benefits for Black and brown communities. We can spark a conversation with our children by asking, "Why do you think people don't have enough food at home?" It's important to always blame the system and not person-blame. If you hear comments like "People are lazy," "Some people don't want to work hard," or other harmful stereotypes, it's your responsibility to disrupt this inaccurate and harmful stereotype. I find this statement helpful: "People don't have enough to eat because our state does not support a livable wage." Another option is saying, "No one chooses to be hungry. But people have to make tough choices like paying for housing or paying for medication. Those tough choices can leave people without the money needed for food." Lastly, drop an "I wonder" statement to cultivate critical thinking skills: "I wonder if it would be possible for everyone in our country to have enough nutritious food to eat," or "I wonder what needs to be done so everyone can have access to nutritious foods."

Individual ways our families can support our neighbors is by regularly donating to the food bank. Make this an active choice, not an afterthought or holiday activity. Think of ways to involve your children, like writing it down on the calendar and asking them to remind you to shop for your neighbors. If your pantry looks more like a bunker, make a donation box in the pantry where they can regularly add to it. Make it someone's job to check the expiration date on all foods before donating—expired foods have no place in the donation bin. On your shopping trips, take your children with you and ask them to personally shop for items.

If you have disposable income and you can give your children a budget to shop with, do that! Cobe loves picking out his favorite items to share with his neighbors. Before you go, check in with your local food pantries and community kitchen to ask what they need. Our school-age children can search on the internet for the list or call them up to find and then shop. Last but not least, support community-owned and people of the global majority–owned grocery stores and your local community fridges.

Grocery Shopping to Reduce Consumption

For those tasked with grocery store shopping, try purchasing in bulk and bringing your own containers and bags. Another tip that works for our family: I limit the pre-cut and pre-packed fruits and vegetables I purchase. Instead, I put the children to work peeling the carrots, slicing the cucumbers, and using the manual food processor to cut the onions when we get home. One more trick that seems to work for me: planning. When our children were under six, I made a commitment to always have a list with me when I shopped. I wanted to model planning for our children, but it also helped me to be present with them instead of trying to remember what I was supposed to buy. Now, before we enter the store, whether it's in the car or at home, I ask if anyone *needs* or *wants* anything. The expectation is that no one can ask for a want in the store but can remind me of any needs. This helped tremendously for us to stay on task and budget.

Beware of Nostalgia and Convenience

Antiracism calls us to live a life full of intentional acts, to come to new understandings and commit to new ways to live justly—not to repeat patterns of oppression. Two of the biggest obstacles to becoming antiracist are nostalgia and convenience. Nostalgia will prohibit us from seeing multiple perspectives, from thinking critically about the harm we are causing because we are centering our own comfort. Choosing to support racist authors, actors, and production companies because we have warm and fuzzy feelings about them is perpetuating racism.

Convenience maintains the status quo, and it deprives us of creativity and our community. Amazon makes it easy to support them over your local bookstore, local grocery store, and almost any other store, but this support of Amazon costs local businesses and artisans. This hasn't been an easy road for us, either. Family members, friends, and coworkers have all questioned our acts. We've been labeled many things, but usually not antiracist. Being antiracist means we choose to put people over profits. We've had to explain many times to our parents that our children will not have long Christmas lists like I did when I was a child. Nor will we make a big fuss about back-to-school shopping for clothes and supplies. Our children are not deprived of living the American dream (or American nightmare, as some call it) of mass consumerism—instead, we are oriented toward the global dream of being conscious citizens living in harmony with the land and our neighbors.

Questions to ask to unpack nostalgia and convenience:

1. Who or what is this about? Is this about me or about my children?
2. What feelings do I associate with this or how does this make me feel?
3. What parts of this activity or purchase are inclusive and what parts are exclusive?
4. How can this be personalized? Is there an artisan I can support instead?
5. What's the true cost of this convenience?
6. Who is paying the cost or at what expense?

Practices

Making Lists of Locally Owned and PoGM-Owned Businesses to Support

For parents, caregivers, and adolescents

It's important to instill the need to support local and PoGM-owned businesses in your children in order for them to better engage in community care and in your shared family values. This activity can be done with your children over time to help them identify the businesses they want to support.

Research: For this step, take a look at what resources are available to you to identify these businesses. There are badge features on yelp .com, for example, that signal whether a business is Black-owned, locally owned and operated, family-owned and operated, minority-owned and operated, and women-owned and operated. There are also badges to help indicate restaurants using locally sourced ingredients. While not perfect (there are plenty of businesses that are/do these things but haven't acquired/requested the badges yet), it's a great place to start your list.

Other sites to check are your local chamber of commerce websites, as well as Buy from BIPOC or Buy from LGBTQ+ websites, organizations, and databases. Many of these websites and databases are still being crafted and are always being updated, so they most often will be incomplete. For larger businesses, you can research who has committed to the 15 Percent Pledge,[16] an organization that works with companies to pledge 15 percent of their shelf space to Black-owned businesses. The 15 Percent Pledge website is also working on creating a database of Black-owned businesses, which aims to be available to consumers soon.

Verify: If you're unsure whether or not a business is locally owned, family-owned, BIPOC-owned, etc., hop onto their website and read their story. Most businesses and restaurants have an About section on their website; use this opportunity to read through their story and get to know the owners, their team, and their history. If you have trouble finding the information you're looking for, don't be afraid to call the business and ask if they're locally owned.

A great question to consider when we think of the term *locally owned* is: Does the family/the owners live in our community? Therefore, will the money come back into our community? Will we be supporting the economic growth and vitality of our community if we shop here?

Create: If there are no databases or lists for these types of businesses in your area, *make* one. You can always keep a Google document and update it over time, but you could also set up a free Wix website or a WordPress blog and document all the local, BIPOC, LGBTQ+, and women-owned businesses and restaurants in your area and publish it so it's an available resource for those in your community. You can even chat with local business owners to inform them about it. Create a social media account dedicated to it. The possibilities are endless! Either way, you're teaching your child to be more engaged with the community and to support local businesses.

Noticing Differences at the Grocery Store

For families with children ages four and older

Since many of us shop at stores that either share our zip code or are easily accessible to us, we limit our exposure to noticing differences and noticing unfairness. For this activity, our aim is to embrace the language of unfairness by exploring different grocery stores in our community, but really you could compare any two stores that are similar. Through acquiring the language of unfairness, noticing the disparity of resources, and learning about lack of access, your family can use your antiracist lens to connect how these differences are related to community inequality. Remember to communicate that a community's resources or aesthetics (or lack thereof) don't equate to that community's value.

1. On your usual shopping trips, start to notice small details about your store with your children. Work to bring your children into the conversation and have them notice with you. Below, you'll find questions to help guide your conversation with the goal of your children leading the way to notice how your grocery store provides for your family.

    a. **In the parking lot:** What's the size of the lot? Are the parking lines visible? How and where does one return carts? Are there parking spaces designed for people expecting a child or for families with small children? Is the lot well-lit? Are there places to sit and eat? What's displayed outside for purchase? How many handicap-accessible parking spaces are available? How far away is the bus stop? Is there a security guard patrolling?

    b. **Before entering:** Do they accept SNAP benefits or WIC coupons? (Most stores will display a sticker in the window or on the entrance door.)

    c. **Inside the store:** Is the store well-lit? Is the floor clean and free of clutter? How does the store smell? Does the store offer additional services like check cashing, coin exchange, or cooking classes?

d. **While shopping:** Is the produce seasonal or does the store offer out-of-season produce? What's the quality of the produce? What produce is new to your children? How is the produce displayed? What's the cost of an orange or apple?

e. Are samples offered for the customers? Does the bakery offer a cookie program for young children? Does your store have a snack corner for young children? Does your store offer stickers or coupons for young children?

f. Is prepared food available to purchase and enjoy? Are hot and cold options available for quick meals? Is there a place for people to sit and enjoy their food inside?

g. Does it have an "ethnic foods" aisle or an aisle meant to represent "global" non-dominant foods and ingredients? Why do you think these types of food/ingredients are limited to just one aisle? How many ingredients are available in the "ethnic foods" aisle? What is considered "ethnic"?

h. **When it's time to check out:** How many cashiers are available? Does your store use baggers? Does the store encourage reusable bags by offering a discount? Does the store offer drive-up for their in-store shoppers?

2. Make a commitment to try other grocery stores with your children that are outside of your neighborhood or zip code. Each time your family explores a new grocery store, choose some of the same questions as those above to notice differences and similarities. Children will naturally compare the two grocery stores with practice. You might hear your child say, "This grocery store doesn't have a self-checkout," or "Where's the children's cart for me?" Encourage your children to continue to notice differences. Some differences will

be just that, a different experience. Other differences will lead to conversations about unfairness, especially when it's the exact same brand of grocery store in two different zip codes.

3. When our children notice unfairness, respond by asking them:

    a. How is this unfair?

    b. Who's being treated differently or unfairly?

    c. What could be offered instead? What is missing?

    d. What can we do about it?

Cultures Are Not Costumes Checklist

For parents, caregivers, and adolescents

Many people in our community love Halloween and the magic of dressing up. Part of creating a safe school community for ALL students on Halloween is making sure racially, ethnically, and culturally based costumes aren't part of our festivities, because cultures are not costumes.

Families are invited to consider the Cultures Are Not Costumes checklist below:

> **Research:** Learn about antiracist practices by reading, watching, and listening to testimonials created by people from communities impacted by cultural appropriation and racism.
>
> **Reflect:** Think about how your family can be a part of ending racism and the cycle of harm caused by cultural appropriation. While some people might not be offended by a racially or ethnically based costume, many people are. Raising empathetic humans means we do not ignore hurt or harm when present; instead, we encourage curiosity, asking questions, and understanding another perspective more fully.
>
> **Discuss:** Talk with your family about what kind of creative costumes you can make or purchase that will avoid cultural appropriation and still feel fun and respectful to wear!
>
> **Act:** Interrupt cultural appropriation by committing to antiracist practices in your home. Appreciating cultures—not appropriating them—takes time, humility, and openness.

Building an antiracist world includes all of us taking action. Let's not get stuck in the sticky web of racism this Halloween; cultures are NOT costumes!

—Emi Ito

Email Template for Companies that Are Committed to Sustainability and Ethical Practices but Lack Racial Justice Consciousness

For parents, caregivers, and adolescents

Subject: Critical Feedback

Hello All,

I recently found your brand and immediately started noting items I would like to purchase, like _____. I can't say thank you enough for building a sustainable business. This is why when I stumbled across your beautiful "kimonos," I knew you all would want to know the language is rooted in unethical behavior. If you're like *Whoa, what?* check out this article by Emi Ito, "An Open Letter to White Makers & Designers Who Are Inspired by the Kimono and Japanese Culture," in which she offers us a history lesson and antidotes to non-Japanese folks like myself:

How do I avoid cultural appropriation of Japanese culture?

- Use terms like *duster, robe, cardigan, wrap coat,* and *drop-sleeve top* rather than *kimono*. The kimono may not be considered a sacred garment to all Japanese-heritage people, but it certainly is to many of us. Do not abuse our sacred, spiritual ties to our garments by appropriating the term.

Since I have no way of knowing if the founders of your company identify as Japanese or partnered with Japanese designers, other than asking, this may not pertain to you.

Please let me know either way.

Sustainable clothing and racial justice are equally important in building the world we want to live in and pass to our children.

Will [name of company] rename your jackets?

I'm hoping this email is met with curiosity, especially since we're not in a relationship with one another, and please know I'm willing to partner with you in any way I can.

I look forward to hearing from you soon,

[Insert name here]

We hope you and your child have learned more about environmentalism, consumption, collective care, and community economics through an antiracist lens, and how these things indeed intersect; none are mutually exclusive. Being conscious about our land, our community, and the capitalist system we're a part of, especially with an antiracist lens, can help change our world for the better by raising the next generation of conscious citizens and antiracists.

thriving communities

Part of being antiracist is shifting your mindset from an individualist one to a collaborative, communal one. You can't be focused on repairing the harm others experience or crafting a more equitable world if you're *only* focused on your own success, struggles, and growth. The American way, the capitalist way, is one of overworked and exploited people with individualistic mindsets. In order to best model collaboration, we should shift away from exploitation and more toward harmony.

In this part, you'll learn how (and why) to raise children that constantly think about, advocate for, and support their neighbors. We'll touch on how to foster considerate, loving friendships, creating homes focused on respect, safety, and authenticity, and building more equitable communities better suited to all their members.

This type of support can manifest in a number of ways: from supporting grassroots movements and local nonprofit charities to protesting inequitable policies and supporting local unions. We'll go into different examples below while also touching on the practices you and your child can commit to in order to be considerate, authentic individuals to all.

At the end of the day, we as antiracists are committed to the outcomes. Teaching your children to keep this in mind will better prepare them to extend compassion when offering criticism to others.

What Is Community?

Community can mean where you physically reside, and it can also mean the people who make up your web of relationships. For our youngest learners, we'll use the terms *family* and *community* interchangeably. Being in a community means we seek to be in harmony with our neighbors, take responsibility for our feelings, and choose to repair harm with our loved ones, friends, and rivals. Above all else, it means holding people and places accountable when they cause harm.

Conflict, disagreements, and obstacles will occur every day in our communities and our relationships. We must understand that those disagreements and conflicts will not (and should not) end relationships, unless of course the relationship is hurting you or causing you harm. This is a huge point for many, but particularly for older learners who often view things in binary terms (right versus wrong, fair versus unfair). Binary thinking oversimplifies the issue and doesn't allow for creative responses. Creative thinking takes time, commitment, and trust, all crucial ingredients to build a strong community and have successful conflicts that result in solutions and repair.

When a relationship fades, a lot of times it wasn't because of a specific conflict. It was because the relationship was neglected, one or both of you withdrew your energy, and the hard work of repairing felt like it was too much. Perhaps there was a loss of trust or safety, and the lack of communication or reconciliation prevented repair.

There are a series of activities we've provided in this part to help your family cultivate a deeper relationship with your people-community. Read up and explore together.

How Inclusive Is Your Universe? How Inclusive Is Your Child's Universe?

I've been on a journey to better define inclusion and why it's important to me. I started by noticing how diverse my particular universe is to realize whether or not it was inclusive. In 2013, I truly thought I was living an inclusive experience because my hometown, Rockford, Illinois, had racial diversity. My understanding of inclusivity at the time was mostly anchored to the idea of racial diversity. I soon realized, however, that inclusion doesn't happen through abstract census data: inclusion is about who we're in community with every day. I had to ask myself:

1. Who was I connecting with?
2. What were the opportunities for diversity and inclusion?
3. How was the city investing in communities of color?
4. What initiatives or laws contributed to racist or antiracist outcomes?

For generations, public and private institutions continued to invest in predominantly white areas while divesting from predominantly Black neighborhoods. In researching more about Rockford, I soon learned my hometown maintained contemporary segregation through local government policies.

My partner and I agreed that if our city wasn't going to help us integrate, it was on us. We got real about what diversity was and wasn't and why it was important to foster inclusion. After several conversations, we made what seemed like a radical but necessary decision (at the time) to move away from our hometown to Houston, Texas, in order to seek, promote, and foster diversity and inclusion in our home.

Ask yourself these same questions when considering your community and your neighborhood. The census data numbers are a place to start, but research further. Are you encountering cultures and ethnicities that are different from yours on a daily basis? Is there notable income inequality? What kind of people are holding power in government, or even in your child's school? When you're dining out, shopping for electronics, or shopping for groceries, notice if there's a racial hierarchy among the staff and managerial positions.

We know why we want our children around diversity: we want the expectation of "normal" to constantly be challenged. We want children to experience all kinds of people doing everyday things. We want them to embrace people, to practice becoming welcomers, and to have an identity based on reality versus superiority or inferiority.

You'll have to decide what actions are necessary (and maybe even radical) to create the diversity you want your family to experience, and the inclusion you want others to experience. This might mean becoming more involved with your community, and it might mean moving out of your community.

There's an activity at the end titled "How Diverse Is Your Universe?" for you to complete. As you do, respond with curiosity and openness. Notice where in your life your family practices inclusion. The goal in this exercise is to just notice. After taking stock of your family's diversity profile, you can begin analyzing how you've created homogeneous or diverse experiences for your children. This analysis offers your family the chance to develop a road map for diversity and inclusion. You'll have the choice to say, "I want to continue this path by doing XYZ" or, "Here's how we're going to make changes to better align our values with our actions."

It should be noted that diversity alone doesn't address inequities, and diversity doesn't mean a group of people automatically are welcomed or accepted in a space. Most important, great harm can still happen in diverse spaces. This is why inclusion and justice are necessary goals.

Affinity Spaces: Safe Environments for Children to Learn and Feel Supported

One way you and your child can learn and connect with other members of your identity group safely is within an **affinity space**. Affinity spaces are where education, relationship building, and support can occur among groups of people that share interests, passions, and characteristics. There can be career or activity affinity spaces, and there can be identity affinity spaces.

There are **white social justice affinity spaces** for committed white folks to constructively come together and learn about racism, antiracism, and social justice while sparing the people of the global majority in their lives the burden of educating them. These folks acknowledge their starting places of learning, unlearning, and action are different from those of the global majority, so they seek out separate spaces to confront the patterns, manifestations, and histories of white domination within themselves and within their communities.

Affinity spaces of color have been a staple of many offices and universities attempting to create safer spaces for people of the global majority to process experiences unique to their racialized identity. While these spaces can also be ones of learning, they're usually ones of processing, healing, community, and support. It's important that white folks don't view affinity spaces of color as exclusionary to them. If you do feel excluded, check in with yourself and investigate that feeling. It's important to not feel entitled here. Remember that these are necessary safer spaces for those who experience forms of discrimination, exclusion, and challenges specific to *them*. Not every space is for everyone. If you're a part of a dominant culture, society is made with you in mind. You're able to take up space everywhere. Remember that marginalized communities are entitled to their own affinity spaces.

Look into joining an affinity space that's right for you and your child. The necessary work of learning and unlearning heavily involves community and accountability, so joining a group committed to the same things will help you succeed on your growth journey. If there are no affinity spaces at your work or in your child's school, inquire about making or hosting one to provide this resource. If you have questions about how to structure or moderate these kinds of affinity groups, there are several websites and online resources available to help you get started. One particular resource is the set of tool kits put together by Racial Equity Tools, all for free.[1]

Finding Our Place: Building a Liberatory Community

The framework I've found most helpful in developing my critical consciousness, analysis, and action is Barbara J. Love's framework for Developing a Liberatory Consciousness. It provides a starting point to "be an effective liberation worker—committed to changing systems and institutions characterized by oppression to create equity and social justice."[2] It's a method for individuals seeking social change. When engaging with the framework, one will feel a sense of responsibility instead of shame. We understand we didn't create the oppressive system and yet we're always being advantaged or disadvantaged by that system. We understand we have the responsibility and power to create different outcomes.

The first stage in the cycle is **awareness**: notice your language, your position, your thoughts, your ideas, your neighbors, your behaviors, and your outcomes. Most important, notice the unfairness and discrimination. Next, before moving to action, **analyze** your choices. What are your values, your goals, and your desired outcomes? How much time do you have to commit, and what are your resources? Once you have a running list of choices, you're ready to take action. **Action** could be taking individual initiatives, supporting others, locating resources, or reminding others it's their work to do. There can also be collective action: working with a team to write policies, participating in a boycott, starting a petition, or organizing a protest. The final step in the process is **accountability/allyship:** *Who are you working with or being accountable to at this moment? How are you creating space for the critical conversations to take place? How are you working to carry your weight in the building of liberation?*

Embracing Conflict

We're going to cut to the chase: we'll have to embrace conflict in order for us to nurture ourselves and our relationships. Conflict is a part of human nature, and it can be healthy, reduce stress, and actually sustain relationships. Unfortunately, white domination has designed for connections to always keep things casual and light, suppressing honest conversations and stark truths.

We must unlearn our fear of open conflict by following our fearless children. "No!" "Stop it!" "That's mine!" These definitive statements are our children advocating for themselves. Telling our loved ones what's rude or disrespectful isn't hurtful, it's necessary.

When I start to overthink how to advocate for myself, I'm reminded of my friend Mel Velez's words, "You already know what to do because it belongs to you." In our home, when a conflict arises, I name it right away: "This sounds like a conflict." I want my children to have language for the activation they feel in their hearts, bodies, and minds. I also want to normalize healthy conflict: "Disagreements can lead to clarity; use your words when you're ready." As parenting partners, how we respond to the conflict will live with our children for years to come and make a profound impact on the ways they advocate for themselves and others. Let's make sure they have the tools to sustain a relationship rather than break one.

Teach your children how to be accountable:

1. Take accountability: "I took your shirt and wore it to school."
2. Repair: "How can I make it better?"
3. Make peace: this could be a hug, a handshake, a high five, or a word. It closes the conflict.

Conflict resolution doesn't have to happen at the moment, either. When we notice our children struggling to breathe, holding back tears, or balling up their fists, call attention to it. Ask your children to release the activation in their bodies before communicating. "Set a timer for twenty minutes and then meet back at the table." Releasing activation might involve running around, rubbing their hands back and forth, drawing, or writing. Our toddlers and preschoolers do this naturally when they throw a temper tantrum. They're releasing tears, which contain cortisol, a stress hormone.

To encourage honesty, independence, and trust, both children involved in a conflict will need to do their part in sharing their side of the story. As the youngest of three, I was often asked by my parents to report what really happened in situations involving my sisters. This continually put me in an awkward position with my sisters and created tension where there had originally been none. With this in mind, resist involving other siblings as "witnesses"; this only adds to the distrust among your children. Also, resist stepping in to "save" your children. This one is tough for me. Instead, I remind my children that I'm nearby. When we teach and expect conflict resolution in our home, we're teaching our children how to advocate for themselves. I invite my children to let me know when they need help or don't feel heard. As adults who fear rocking the boat, these are good practices for you, too. Conflicts can be so healing for ourselves and our relationship. When we practice accountability, repairing harm, and conflict resolution in our home, we can extend the practices into our friendships, too.

How to Nurture Ourselves and Our Cross-Racial Relationships

How can we be friends if I don't feel comfortable sharing the racist remark another customer said to me, or worse, the racist statement you made to me? How can we be friends if I'm overly focused on your comfort and defensiveness? How long will our relationship sustain when my stories of racism are too heavy for you to hear? I ask these honest questions of my antiracist white friends because we both want a relationship that holds space for all of our experiences shaped by our identities. We want relationships where we're our full selves with one another.

Consider: How are you preparing and modeling for your children to have cross-racial friendships? As we build our antiracist future, we're building a future where integration and accountability is expected and encouraged. We know that by thirty months, race can become a determinant for children when choosing playmates.[3] To challenge this, we must prepare our home where cross-racial friendships are seen and modeled. When your children are around five years old, begin having explicit conversations. For example, show them a picture of two friends, one white and one Black, and say, "Look at these friends playing." Make it known that they can be friends with those who look different from them. Be intentional about the representation of friendship you're exposing your child to.

Preparing our children for cross-racial friendships requires us to explicitly discuss racism, prejudice, and bias as a family. It's important that our children feel comfortable asking us questions about these topics. Research shows explicit conversations with five- to seven-year-olds about interracial friendship can dramatically improve racial attitudes in as little as a single week.[4] It's also important for children to know that they might make mistakes in the cross-racial friendship, and that making those mistakes isn't the end of the world. Focus on learning, unlearning, and repair.

How Can Children Support Friends Who Just Experienced Racism (or Any Identity-Group-Based Discrimination)?

In a cross-racial friendship, usually one person has more immunity than the other. It is up to the person with more immunity to step up and advocate for their more vulnerable friend.

When the Coronavirus pandemic was at its initial height, I knew Carter would be hearing anti-Chinese rhetoric at school. I wanted to have a discussion with Carter about this so he could be best prepared to advocate for others if the need to do so arose. The first step we needed to take was fully understanding the problem that's occurring in our larger society. After discussing, we both agreed that Chinese Americans were being unfairly attacked, dehumanized, and blamed for the Coronavirus outbreak, and therefore could use support from allies and friends.

The next step Carter and I worked on was vocabulary. I pulled some words for him to learn or review so that our conversation would be as accessible to him as possible. As an example, here are some of the terms I pulled:

1. racism
2. prejudice
3. anti-Chinese
4. xenophobic
5. Coronavirus
6. COVID-19
7. microaggressions

Then, after reviewing each definition, we made a cloud graph with the word *dehumanize* at the center. Together, we free-associated *racist remarks*, *othering*, *microaggression*, and *un-American*—all words and terms he either heard secondhand or had read in recent articles. After discussing each word and its meaning, we then searched for examples of each of these free-associated aggressions in articles we read together.

After this writing exercise, Carter and I had a serious conversation about his responsibility to speak up and advocate for anyone experiencing Sinophobia at school. Some people say, "Sticks and stones may break my bones but words will never hurt me." We know this statement isn't true. Those prejudiced words are used to uphold white domination by justifying disrespecting another human being, normalizing racism, and in this case, keeping Chinese people viewed as "othered." I asked Carter, "When we continually see Chinese people as 'othered' or not American (enough), what discriminatory policies can be easily enacted? How does this uphold white domination?" The Chinese Exclusion Act, the Geary Act, and the Queue Ordinance of 1873 are just a few.

Together, Carter and I then came up with the following agreements (inspired by Learning for Justice's "Speak Up at School" activity):[5]

Interrupt: I'll speak up against biased statements—every time, in the moment, no exception. I'll say things like, "We do not use that phrase." If someone mocks the Chinese language, I'll say, "Don't do that, it's rude."

Question: I'll ask why the person made the comment. "Can you explain the joke to me?" or "What do you mean by that?" I'll ask them, "Would you like it if someone said that to you?"

Educate: I'll explain why what they said is offensive. Sometimes ignorance is the cause of the harmful behavior, or lack of exposure to a diverse population. "You're making a hurtful generalization about this person because of their race. That's rooted in racism."

Echo: If someone else speaks up, I'll thank them and reiterate their sentiment. "You're right, Maliah. That's unkind, bro."

There are multiple ways for children to advocate against discrimination. If the situation involves one or a few people, they can use the skills above to advocate on an individual scale. Sometimes this type of advocacy can look like speaking up and saying something to the person causing harm, and sometimes advocacy can look like standing beside the person who's being harmed. Depending on the situation, advocacy can also look like going to an authority figure, like a teacher or a parent, to help defuse and facilitate a situation and plan next steps.

If dealing, for example, with a larger-scale issue, such as a racist policy or a racist textbook, children can engage with collective activism. This could look like participating in a boycott, signing a petition, or engaging in another type of organized effort. At this scale, your child will be one of many demanding change; it is by no means work to do alone.

Making and maintaining cross-racial friendships through adolescence means white children will need to learn how to listen to stories of racism and how to support their friends of the global majority through racist incidents. Dr. Beverly Daniel Tatum is an expert in child and adolescent racial-ethnic identity development. In an interview with *HuffPost*, she shares: "If a white child has a friend of color, it's likely that the friend is a minority in a mostly white community. . . . Then, as those friends of color approach adolescence, they start to become aware of experiences with racism, from name-calling and racial profiling in stores or by police, to social exclusion—not being invited to teenage birthday parties, for instance. . . . If the child of color is being teased or excluded, and the white friend doesn't speak up, or worse, participates in the teasing or excluding, 'the cross-racial friendship will eventually unravel.'"[6]

With this in mind, here are five steps you can break down for your child to support their friends:

1. When your friend says they've just experienced group-based discrimination, **acknowledge** and (most important) **believe** what they said and experienced.
2. **Hold space** for them to process their feelings out loud. Let them take their time.
3. **Ask** how you can best show up for them and support them at this moment.
4. With permission from your friend, **amplify** what they said by telling a relevant adult (teacher, parent, guardian, etc.) about the experience, or even sharing their message on social media.
5. **Remind them** that they're loved.

Modeling Asking for and Providing Pronouns

In order to have thoughtful, authentic relationships, we must constantly be considerate of the identities of others. This goes beyond race: as antiracists pursuing liberation, we don't just stop at race, we consider sexuality, gender, abilities, and other identity facets with great care. It's also important to note that queer and trans folks of color are even more at risk due to the multiple intersecting minoritized identities that they hold. In this way and in many others, being thoughtful about gender and sexuality is a fundamental antiracist practice. As discussed in Part One, our intersecting identities inform and relate to one another, as well as impact how we exist and are viewed by the world. Justice isn't just for heterosexual, cisgender, able-bodied people of the global majority. Liberation is for everyone. We should not and cannot separate antiracism from gender justice.

As touched on in Part Two, when introducing this topic with children, start by talking about **gender** and **gender expression**. For example, someone could identify as a man or as nonbinary, and that would be their gender. This person could choose to wear dresses, makeup, and jewelry and have long hair, and these are forms of gender expression. While these acts of gender expression for this person might come across as "feminine" to some, this in no way negates how that person identifies. What does this lesson teach us? You can't assume pronouns or gender identity just by looking at someone; we should ask them to be sure.

How to Introduce Yourself in a Gender-Inclusive Way

After breaking down these concepts for your child, model asking for someone's pronouns when first introduced, and encourage your child to do the same. The best way to ask for someone's pronouns is to offer up yours. By opening the conversation with your pronouns, you show that you're open, respectful, and welcoming by putting yourself out there first. You're indicating that you're familiar with pronouns and that the person can trust you to be considerate about them. For example:

> "Hi there, I'm Tasha. I use *she/her* pronouns."
> "Hello, I'm Ari, and I use gender-neutral pronouns, such as *they, them,* and *theirs.*"
> "Hi! I'm Ruby, and my pronouns are *she* and *they.*"
> "Hey! I'm Robin. You can call me R or Robin."

Sometimes, folks will respond by introducing themselves and their pronouns, but sometimes they just might say their name. That's an opportunity to follow up and say, "If you feel comfortable sharing, what are your pronouns?" The more natural and warm you are, the safer and more respected the other person will feel. If a person responds in a challenging way by saying something like, "Can't you tell?" or "What are you even talking about?" don't be discouraged. Instead, let them know that you don't want to ever misgender someone by assuming, so asking for pronouns ensures you're affirming the person.

At the doctor's office, at a new school, or any other time your children might need to identify their pronouns, don't assume—things might have changed since the last time you spoke with them. Children discover more about their gender and their sexuality as they grow, so checking in with them about their pronouns more than once over time provides them the space to change and explore. Together you can notice when pronouns aren't asked for on an information sheet, find space on the sheet, and write them in together. Another way to make pronouns more visible is by writing them on name tags. You're modeling this for your children so your children know to follow your example.

How to Apologize After Misgendering

Misgendering is when someone uses a pronoun or form of address for a person that doesn't correctly reflect their identified gender. Sometimes this can happen by mistake, and sometimes people do it on purpose as an act of transphobic violence. Either way, when misgendering occurs, it's an act of harm. Knowing that it's harmful, if we ever misgender someone, we must apologize, no matter how unintentional the act was. Mistakes happen, but that doesn't mean we can ignore them when they do.

One thing to note when apologizing is that it should be quick and heartfelt, but shouldn't go on and on. The moment you begin negative self-talk out loud to the person you misgendered, you force them into the position of comforting you when they're the one who just experienced the harm. This overdrawn apology can get especially awkward if both of you are with other people.

If you slip up, simply say, "I'm sorry, I meant to say (insert correct pronoun)." That's it; quick and sincere is best. If they themselves correct you, avoid defensiveness and receive it as a gift: "I'm so sorry about that. Thanks for correcting me!" If you want, you can also apologize in private after the fact: "Hey, I'm really sorry I misgendered you earlier. Thanks for being patient with me. I truly value your feedback."

What's also helpful is to default to gender-neutral pronouns when meeting or hearing about someone new. For example, if you're at a party and someone asks, "Hey, have you had a chance to talk with Piper?" you can respond with, "No, I haven't had the chance to meet them yet." The use of considerate gender-neutral language like this saves others from assumptions.

Lastly, when referring to a group of people, try to stay away from gendered forms of address. Use gender-neutral language when referring to folks you don't know who haven't had the chance to self-identify to you yet. For example, "Congrats on getting married! I'd love to meet your partner," or "Is it true that your sibling is graduating from high school tomorrow?" For your children, encourage them to use gender-neutral alternatives to *boy* and *girl* for anyone they don't know, such as "That kid's wearing an orange shirt" instead of "That boy has an orange shirt." Another instance could be "That person has a dog" versus "That lady has a dog."

Other examples of gender-neutral address are:

"Welcome, distinguished guests!" instead of "Good evening, ladies and gentlemen."

"Hey, y'all," or "Hey, everyone," instead of "Hey, guys."

"Good morning, students!" instead of "Good morning, boys and girls!"

"What can I get you folks today?" instead of "What can I get you ladies today?"

How to Interrupt and Correct Someone Else

To be an active ally, you must advocate for others who are more vulnerable. If someone is being misgendered, it could feel difficult and painful for that person to correct others on their own behalf. As an active ally, you have a responsibility to speak up. One way to do this is: "I have to interrupt. Mark, you've misgendered alex twice now. A reminder that their pronouns are *they* and *them.*" Continue to use the correct pronouns for the individual as much as possible in the conversation so that others hear and understand.

Modeling Self-Compassion and Extending Compassion

Compassion is pivotal to antiracist work. As caregivers, we're constantly unlearning harmful lessons and stereotypes in order to be more aware and more conscious. We experience shame, guilt, and embarrassment about past actions (and sometimes even current ones). The emotional difficulties and reactions of unintentionally harming another are completely normal, and they're a positive sign: by experiencing them, you recognize that what's been done isn't right, and you know that your behavior needs to change. With this in mind, we should constantly consider compassionate forms of communication, expression, and existence when either being challenged or challenging others to do better.

Modeling Self-Compassion

When you first point out patterns of behavior or thought in your children rooted in racism or any other group-based discrimination, your child might feel embarrassment, guilt, or shame. Once again, feelings like this are typical. What's important is that they don't cause the child to shut down or panic. This is important for two reasons. The first is that learning and unlearning behavior and thought patterns will continue throughout their lives. This will happen when they're given the gift of truth by being informed or challenged by those around them. When you notice your children shutting down, try asking them, "What do you need so you can make peace with your younger self?" We want them to trust who they're becoming. Remember, the goal is progress, not perfection.

The second reason is that by panicking, shutting down, or the like, the child is centering *their* feelings versus the harm they caused another (however unintentional) and the repair they need to provide. When centering the self happens and children try to place blame or responsibility elsewhere by saying "He started it" or "I didn't think . . ." Respond firmly with "We're going to let the truth take up space" or "Let's come back to this when you've forgiven yourself."

We can encourage children away from this pattern with two shifts in thought:

1. As mentioned in our Note to Parents, **encourage them to think of feedback, honesty, and vulnerability as gifts:** "Thank you so much for giving me the gift of truth so I can continue to grow. I appreciate you." If you've been given the gift of truth or challenged by another to be better, that person did so because they believe you *can* be better. They've given you the gift of knowledge, awareness, and trust by doing so, and that's a wonderful thing: "Thank you for taking care of me. I have the ability to change my behavior and I will."

2. **Encourage them to have self-compassion.** Treat yourself with the same compassion, understanding, and kindness you'd give to a friend who felt down about their own shortcomings. My go-to phrase here is: "You *made* a mistake. You aren't the mistake." Learning and growing involve pains; maybe it was learning to swim, learning to tie your shoes, learning a second language, or long division that caused you

pain. All learning requires us to make mistakes, and racial justice work isn't any different. What's important is that we continue to try to be better. If your child exhibited behavior that was unfair or problematic, that doesn't make them a bad person. What's important is that they apologize, work on repairing the harm they caused, and do better next time. Work with your child to identify ways they can provide themselves momentary care to stop the spiral of cruel self-criticism while staying engaged and thankful to those that critiqued them.

It's not just children who have trouble navigating these difficult feelings; adults struggle with wrestling with their guilt and shame all the time. Modeling that you think of being challenged to do better as a gift will instill in your children the same understanding. Modeling self-compassion will teach your children to not be cruel to themselves for failing momentarily.

Extending Compassion to Others

Once we begin our own antiracist work and start disrupting behavior and challenging those we come across to be better, we must aim for compassionate accountability. This isn't about gaining awareness to one-up on someone, it's about collective liberation. Therefore, we need accountability. But there's a range of accountability: if the accountability is too compassionate, no growth truly happens in order to preserve comfort and chaos ensues. On the other end of the spectrum, if there's accountability where there's not *enough* compassion, it can cause the relationship you're trying to improve to deteriorate. No one wants to be in a relationship where they feel like they have to be perfect. What this spectrum tells us is that compassion has a lot of power, so much so that it can make or break a relationship. This happens when we're more committed to being right than to moving forward together. When bettering our relationships and our communities, we should aim for a balance of what Samuel Simmons, LADC, refers to as "compassionate accountability."

I use the OAR method when I'm preparing for a critical conversation. OAR stands for Outcome, Action, and Relationship.

Try this method out for yourself. How would you respond if your mother said, "If Black people want the job, they should be professional, cut their hair, and talk right"?

Start with the outcome in mind. What do you want out of this conversation, or what are you hoping will change by having this conversation? The outcomes will inform the actions you take to achieve the goal. Last, but certainly not least, think about the relationship with the person and commit to following up with them after the conversation. Remember, speaking the truth won't hurt the relationship, but disengaging from the person will cause the relationship to fizzle.

Here's an example for the scenario above:

O: People have the right to be employed regardless of their dialect and hairstyle.

A: I will (1) research the word *professional* to better understand its roots, (2) understand how language is learned and shared, (3) understand how whiteness is favored in employment settings, (4) speak with my mother about her comment—"People have the right to be employed regardless of their dialect and hairstyle," and (5) reinforce my belief and desired outcome.

R: After the conversation(s), I'll invite my mother to chat on the phone. I'll also make an effort to bring her coffee or a muffin the next day.

Compassionate accountability expects me to stay engaged in the relationship while still sharing the truth. Tough conversations can leave people feeling vulnerable and defensive. Compassion can help create a sense of safety and prove to others that you're invested in their growth.

Building Relationships

Building relationships is imperative to collective care and antiracist work. We've talked about friendship agreements and guidelines for children, so now we'll dive into building relationships with their home, community, and neighbors. Your child's family is the very first community they're exposed to. In this community, they learn what's valued, what type of communication is successful, who has power and why, and what is and isn't taboo behavior. By inviting children to be active parts of their family's traditions, and by teaching them to consider and create for others, you encourage them to begin thinking and caring beyond the self. When doing the following activities with your child, encourage the view that through beautifying and nurturing a space or a tradition, they're nurturing a community and its people.

1. **Planting and Gardening:** Creating and maintaining a garden with your child can be a way they learn about the effort required to make food, and how precious the accessibility of food sources and green spaces can be. It also shows that in order to help things progress, there must be constant attention and care bestowed to the project at hand. If you or your child stops watering, pruning, or fertilizing your garden, plants can wither and weeds can overrun. Here, responsibility can be given and efforts can visibly bloom. This project can help add nuance and appreciation to your child's relationship with your home, food, and nature, and teach them about commitment and conviction.

2. **Plan a Celebration:** Together, you and your child can work on making a home or neighborhood celebration for a spiritual and/or special holiday (e.g., Juneteenth, Earth Day, May Day, or Labor Day

celebrations) that involves how they want to celebrate. If there will be food, plan the menu together and teach them how to help you cook parts of the meal. If there will be music, make a playlist together. Decorate together, host together. Teach them the meaning not only of the holiday but of your family's (or neighborhood's) celebratory tradition. Help them understand that by being part of your family, they get to influence and add to that tradition.

3. **Host a Game Night:** Introduce your favorite games to your child and have them introduce their favorite games to you. Host a game night where everyone gets together and plays together. Try to include games that are cooperative as well as games that are competitive so that children can experience working together with family members as well as strategic, creative thinking on their own. Be sure to not make unilateral decisions about what to play or listen to, or how to structure the night. Communicate with one another and collaborate on how to best reach the goal of mutual fun and satisfaction. Ask your child, "Are we being fair to everyone's wants and needs tonight?"

Other forms of relationship-building can come from tending to your space (group spring cleaning, rearranging furniture together, folding laundry together), tending to and interacting with the community (creating a scavenger hunt for your child and their neighbors, going to community open mics, working on a mural together), and tending to the land (picking up trash at the beach, planting in community gardens or local parks). These low-cost activities help children build these relationships with their family, their home, and their community.

What Do Our Communities Need, and How Do Privilege, Immunity, and Bias Prevent Access?

In order to have thriving communities for everyone, not just some, we must first acknowledge the systemic inequalities that prohibit resources, access, and equity for people of the global majority. Earlier in the book, we discussed collective care and many of its facets. In this section, we'll talk about how collective care can be used to better our communities and help shift the status quo. As we enjoy our community, here are three foundational questions we can continue to ask our children:

1. Who is here/present?
2. Who is missing or underrepresented?
3. What do you notice is fair or unfair?

As you read through the following sections, continue to return to these questions with your children.

Neighborhood Segregation

Racial segregation contributes to the continued reduced economic growth for millions of people of the global majority today. It also contributes to the continued racial segregation that exists in many of our schools, child-care camps, and recreational programs.

We can notice and call out racial segregation with six- to nine-year-olds. When you enter a new space, notice who's present and who's missing. One summer, I signed my children up for a free community STEM program. While waiting for the program to start, I asked them, "Who do you notice is here and who do you notice is missing?" Without missing a beat, Cobe said, "I haven't seen any white kids." This awareness-building allows us to have an honest conversation about diversity or the lack of diversity. If we notice the lack of diversity or accessibility at an event, we can brainstorm ways the organizers could have attempted to create more inclusion. Then move to action by sharing your family's suggestions to help improve future events.

> Redlining is the deliberate creation of policies and laws that deny services to residents of communities based on race.

With ten- to thirteen-year-olds, briefly research redlining and introduce its definition and history to your child, then take a look at the racial makeup of your city and your neighborhood. Ask the following questions:

1. "Do you notice whether certain areas are still largely racially segregated?"
2. Watch for the ways bias may have already set in your child by asking, "Do you hear people refer to certain areas as good or bad? How about nice or sketchy?"
3. "Do you notice the impacts of gentrification?"

If you live in a community with historic redlining, identify the "color line" with your children. Have conversations with your parenting partners about the efforts from your local government to reduce barriers and create more economic fairness. Seek and support local organizations attempting to dismantle structural racism in housing.

Food, Safety, and Transportation

We all need food, some form of shelter, and the ability to get back and forth between the two. In order for a community to thrive, its members need access to these pivotal resources. However, not everyone has this. These are big topics to discuss with our budding antiracists. A key idea to share with your child is: "Every human being deserves safety, food, shelter, and transportation." To start the conversation about safety, access, and transportation, you can ask:

1. "Do you have a place where you feel safe?"
2. "Do you feel safe in your neighborhood?"
3. "What do you need to feel safe?"

When you introduce how your community works to your child, bring their experiences into the conversation. Are they able to get to and from school efficiently and safely? Is your family able to go to the grocery store with ease if something is needed last minute? If the answer is no, it's important to let your child know it's because the city or state isn't investing in affordable and accessible transportation and housing. As always, introduce the inequities with your child with the language *fair* and *unfair* through a shared antiracist lens.

Food Equity

After hearing some of Carter's friends make comments about people who use food stamps, we started to have conversations about food equity. It was important to introduce definitions casually before practicing concrete activities.

Here's the language we use to introduce these concepts to children: **Food inequity** is when people are living without enough nutritious foods and safe water to maintain healthy physical, mental, and general health. This might be because people live in a **food desert**, an area that has limited access to affordable, safe, and nutritious food and water. People living in a food desert will have to travel more than one mile to access a grocery store, community-supported agriculture

(CSA), or food market. This makes it even more difficult if people don't have access to transportation. They might live in a **food swamp**, areas of town inundated with fast-food restaurants, convenience stores, and high-calorie foods. What we want is for each person to have access to highly nutritious foods in their community regardless of race, income, education, zip code, or age. A final note about these terms: While widely used and accepted, we still feel there's a level of avoidance housed within them. As Germaine Jenkins said: "Food desert is more palatable, but food apartheid is what it is. It's by design." Always remember that these inequities were intentional. They are built into the very structure of our cities. Our goal as a people should be food justice.

It was so important that I give my children the tools to think critically about social services so they can interrupt classist language. In our home we've filled out food stamp applications, calculated the cost of food stamp benefits, walked to the closest grocery store in the Houston heat, and shopped for dinner on a limited budget. These activities were not meant to be a fun adventure or to pity those experiencing food inequity; instead they were meant for us to understand the systemic issue so we could better advocate.

Green Spaces

As discussed in Part Four, environmental racism impacts people of the global majority greatly, especially in terms of toxicity, as pollution disproportionately affects people of the global majority. But there are also several redlining policies that further environmental racism, which in turn affects community health. Notice how minoritized communities face environmental racism: Are the parks smaller (or is there a lack of green spaces altogether)? Do communities of color receive regular trash pickup, lawn care, and pest control? What's the quality of playground equipment in their green spaces, and are they accessible? Contextualize your learning with what research supports: green spaces in under-resourced communities are usually less accessible and of poorer quality than those in areas that are predominantly white.[7] But let's not get stuck in awareness, let's move to action.

With your family, discuss who usually uses these spaces and why. Consider the barriers that exist and brainstorm action items your family can take together to create and advocate for green spaces. Every major metropolitan city has a green initiative; it's up to us to make sure it's reducing environmental racism and contributing positively to under-resourced, Black, and brown communities. Can you volunteer? Can you write to local municipalities to advocate for better policies? Can you donate? What are the ways you can make an impact?

Accessible Playgrounds

Early in our homeschooling journey, Cobe and I would explore new parks in the city. One day we stumbled across a multiservice community center that had an indoor gym and outdoor playground. No one was in the gym when we entered, so Cobe started dribbling a basketball and shooting around. After a few minutes, an employee approached us and asked if either one of us was disabled or had disabilities. Confused, I replied with a quick no. He then explained that this site is for disabled people only, but we were more than welcome to play on the inclusive playground outside. Cobe's five-year-old heart was crushed and my embarrassment grew. As I was gathering our things, Cobe told me how it was unfair that he couldn't play since there wasn't anyone inside and he was following the rules. I forced myself to move through my feelings of embarrassment, defensiveness, and entitlement so I could think clearly about the situation:

1. In this situation, what do I feel/think is unfair?
2. Who holds the dominant identity in this situation?

3. Who holds the marginalized identity in this situation?
4. What places can I access without limitation?
5. What places can disabled people access without limitation?
6. After processing the rest of the questions, I asked myself again: what's really unfair?

Running through these questions helped me have an honest conversation with Cobe. "Cobe, how many gyms are made for your abilities? How many are made for people with disabilities?" As he thought about this question, I said, "We could hop in our car and literally go to any other gym and play. What's really not fair about this situation?" On the way to the outside playground, Cobe and I started to unpack our ableism and entitlement to recognize the actual obstacles and discrimination disabled folks face. Following up, we also spoke about affinity spaces and why it's important for disabled people and people with disabilities to have access to them.

By the time we made it to the outside playground, Cobe and I were in a good place about what had just happened. Before I knew it, he was off meeting new friends. Accessible play spaces are vital. Green spaces and playgrounds are important places of socialization, development, and learning for children, so it's pivotal to have inclusive spaces available for all children. Now, Cobe regularly plays at accessible playgrounds, where he has the opportunity to play with children of various abilities. Talk with your child about the green spaces and play spaces you frequent, and when you do, talk about how accessible, clean, and large the spaces are. Compare these spaces to others in different communities they might have frequented. Does the child notice any unfairness? Remind them that until public spaces are inclusive, communities are not just.

Community Health Organizations

Community health organizations, such as clinics, are nonprofit health-care centers that provide services to their designated communities or neighborhoods. Typically, their mission is to improve the quality of life of their community by offering quality health care, usually while being culturally informed and financially accessible to those with lower incomes. Many local clinics have bilingual employees to support their diverse client base, and many clinics also focus on advocacy, client financial support, and community engagement.

For many, CHOs are the only way they can afford or access health care. CHOs also offer a sense of engagement, equity, and care that many don't feel they receive from larger hospitals. With the lasting effects of redlining, many CHOs are founded in particular neighborhoods because there are no adequate health-care options nearby by design. Many underserved and under-resourced communities truly rely on CHOs, so their funding and community support are crucial to their success.

As antiracists, one of our goals is to support any organization that provides affordable and accessible health-care services to those who need it. Remind your children that all people deserve health and safety. If there's a lack of public health resources in your community, look into volunteering, donating, and organizing for those health services.

As an exercise, talk to your children about your neighborhood and the health-care resources available to them:

1. If you get hurt, is there a hospital nearby you can get to easily?
2. When you go to the doctor, is there someone who's able to speak your language and who treats you with respect?
3. What about your friends and their neighborhoods: do they have access to the same health care and support that you do?

How many questions were you and your child able to answer confidently? Do you and your child notice you have access to these resources, or a lack of them?

Another exercise you can do with your children is a Google Maps exercise. Sit with them and search for the hospitals and urgent care centers in your neighborhood. After marking these institutions, you and your child can call the front desks to ask:

1. Do they take self-pay or Medicaid patients?
2. Are doctors and nurses provided translation services for any hard-of-hearing patients or patients who don't speak English?
3. Is the building accessible to disabled folks or folks without forms of transportation? Do they offer shuttle services?

Public Libraries

I love books so much that Cobe's baby shower theme was children's books. I asked that each person bring a book to donate to his home collection. By the time Cobe was one year old, he owned over fifty beautiful books. As time went on, I collected more books for our home. A couple of years later, my partner challenged my shopping habits and individualism. "When I was little, my mom would always take me to the public library. I loved it there," he recalled. Admittedly, I thought of the public library as a place to occasionally visit for an author talk or to check out a reference book, not a source of community, support, and invaluable resources. My shopping habits were upholding individualism by only buying and hoarding books for our home collection without supporting our public library.

Public libraries are a vital part of our neighborhoods. There have been numerous studies that indicate patrons believe their public libraries contribute to their financial, mental, and emotional well-being, as well as generally support the prosperity of their communities.

They're social hubs that provide free educational programs, resources, and workspaces for telecommuters and students, and offer free internet access and computer usage for those looking for employment, doing research projects, or just looking to browse and stay connected. Through their very ethos, libraries are stewards of sustainability and history. They offer children services such as story time, tailored book lists, yoga classes, music classes, and craft hours. For antiracists looking to support free, relevant programs and resources available to their community members, especially children, supporting the public library is a no-brainer.

Together as a family, make a list of your favorite books by Black authors, Indigenous authors, and other authors of color. Check your library's database to check if the books are available; if not, fill out a request form. Depending on the library, you may be able to donate your books, too. Don't be afraid to ask your public library what's the best way to support them. If you have additional disposable income, offer to pay for another family's late fees. Ask if the children's area needs toys, headphones, or tablets you could donate. Consider speaking to your local librarians to have antiracist educational programs for your community, too. Help them partner with community organizations/organizers to help build personal connections while educating.

Public Swimming Pools and Community Centers

Much like public libraries, community centers help build strong and inclusive community bonds, and generate opportunities for social interaction, collective care, and civic engagement. Free or low-cost after-school and weekend programs are provided to help educate and encourage play, and the buildings themselves provide a safe place to gather, learn, and connect.

Public pools offer many of these same services: they create opportunities for social interactions and new friendships. Some public pools (as well as some community centers) offer free or low-cost swim lessons and water workout classes as well. For those neighbors of ours who don't have pools of their own, being able to access a community one gives their family the opportunity to escape the heat, practice swimming, make friends, and have fun. For families concerned about overcrowding and access, demand more public pools and community centers.

The history and lasting impacts of racism and segregation on public pools can't be ignored, either. After the Civil Rights Act desegregated public spaces and accommodations, local governments adopted new strategies to maintain segregation. For example, some public pools installed membership clubs and "began to charge fees, which acted as a barrier to filter out those pool managers felt were 'unfit.'"[8] Over time, local governments consistently defunded their public recreation facilities, with the lasting impact of leaving folks most under-resourced with little or no access to these amenities. What this shows is that as integration initiatives increased, the funding of public spaces decreased. Consequently, public resources and services like community centers and public pools are often underfunded and under-resourced. In order to have clean, safe, welcoming spaces dedicated to our community, we must provide support in whatever ways we can and speak up about the deterioration of these community staples.

Getting Started

Want to change and better your community? Begin with all of the things going right. Help your children see themselves as community members or citizens who both contribute and receive. Here's a quote from the wonderful Mister Rogers: "All of us, at some time or other, need help. Whether we're giving or receiving help, each one of us has something valuable to bring to this world. That's one of the things that connects us as neighbors—in our own way, each one of us is a giver and a receiver."[9]

While on your daily commutes, name public places, organizations, stores, and people who positively contribute to your community. Eventually you can play an "I notice" game, finding people and places that make your community strong. Depending on where you live, these places or people could be your favorite museum, your teachers, postal workers, the local barbershop, or community activists—all are examples of the abundance and power of your community.

Then you can shift the conversation toward your family. Together, notice how your family contributes or shares. For example: We share books with our neighbors at the local library, we pick up trash to make the playground safer for young children, and we contribute supplies to our local food distribution site, which provides meals to our community. It's important for children to understand the importance of social services, public institutions, and everyday people working to realize an antiracist democracy.

Modeling Collaboration: Volunteering for Organizations that Support PoGM Lives and Issues

Reframing volunteering as a form of communal collaboration is a wonderful way to encourage your child to further invest in collective care. Volunteering makes communities strong and makes connections personal. Through the act of volunteering as collaboration, we constantly keep in mind that we're acting as compassionate antiracist community members. We also stay vigilant that we do not create a superiority complex by keeping in mind *why* we're volunteering. In our home, we often refer to volunteering as "showing up." It's our duty to show up for our neighbors; it's our responsibility to care for each other. That doesn't make us superior or better if we do so: it makes us responsible and committed community members. Our broken social system often leads to folks having to rely on volunteering and volunteers, so by participating in this form of communal collaboration, we address systemic inequities and support our communities.

The Impact of Policing

With the increased visibility of social justice movements against police brutality, many children are turning to adults to help them understand the relationship between racism and policing. Any prior exposure children have to police violence differs greatly between homes, schools, and neighborhoods: children of the global majority may have already witnessed a family member's negative encounter with police, or live in a neighborhood that's regularly patrolled. Unfortunately, many children of the global majority, especially Black and brown children, have had negative experiences with police themselves. For some kids, conversations about police and race are introduced for the first time after learning about a recent protest or incident on the news. Many Black and brown children, however, have frank conversations with their caregivers from a very young age about how they need to act, walk, talk, and acquiesce to police demands in order to come out of an encounter alive. There is a sense of urgency the parents of Black and brown children might feel that the parents of white children might be spared from.

One way to introduce the way policing negatively impacts Black and brown folks is to ask children whether or not they notice the police's presence in their neighborhood, and what specifically they notice:

1. Do they patrol frequently?
2. Do they get to know the community members they patrol?
3. You can also ask your children big questions like "Why do we need police?" or "What are jails for?"

In order for us to have a whole conversation about policing, we have to discuss prisons and mass incarceration. Our goal is to disrupt three dominant narratives most children learn by age seven: (1) police are always here to protect us, (2) jail is for people who do bad things, and (3) kids don't go to jail. Organizations like Wee The People, a Boston-based social justice project for children ages four to twelve, host workshops like "What Are Jails For: The Story of Mass Incarceration" that can help you to navigate conversations about prison, policing, and power.[10] For our thirteen-and-older crowd, The Equal Justice Initiative offers comprehensive resources highlighting the state of mass incarceration for youth. Parenting partners and teenagers can read *Just Mercy* by Bryan Stevenson, and then read *Race to Incarcerate: A Graphic Retelling* by Marc Mauer and Sabrina Jones on their own time.

There's a long history of addressing "problems" in communities of color, such as illiteracy, unemployment, houselessness, and mental illness, disproportionately through the criminal legal system. Mental health issues and chemical addictions are public health issues, not criminal issues, yet Black and brown folks aren't typically given the same consideration, care, or humanity that other communities receive due to bias and racism. This leads to routine police calls that end with the death of an unarmed Black or brown person (for example, according to ProPublica, Black boys ages fifteen to nineteen are twenty-one times more likely to be shot and killed by the police than their white peers).[11] With this in mind, you might be wondering as antiracists how to best work around relying on police in order to address potential concerns while working in solidarity to keep communities safer for all their members. Talking to children about who they can turn to for help is essential to help make these alternatives the norm.

1. First, ask yourself if the issue is merely an inconvenience, or if it's actually serious enough to warrant addressing. Remember, you can't

control how the police will respond, but you can control whether you engage the police. For example, your neighbors are having a party late at night and it's very loud. Can you knock on their door and ask them politely to keep it down? Always remember that your idea of safety (police) might be someone else's reality of danger.

2. If you do need to address the situation, is it something you can do one-on-one, or will you need a friend, neighbor, or family member to join you for support?

3. Is the situation too sensitive for you to handle? For example, do you think domestic violence is occurring next door? If so, could you contact a professional that isn't a police officer instead, such as a domestic abuse hotline or organization with trained professionals? (Below, there will be a list of suggested resources you and your child can review.)

4. If an item has been stolen, is it possible for you to go down to a police station instead of bringing the police into your neighborhood?

Typically, police aren't trained to address mental health or substance use situations, so calling them can lead to arrests or escalations, rather than medical treatment. Many women have communicated feeling ignored or not believed by police after a sexual or physical assault, too. For alternative resources to address these types of situations, there are a number of sites and databases you can reference for your particular area. Dontcallthepolice.com is a database of community-based alternatives to the police by city, although at the time of writing, the database is still being added to and updated, and isn't as comprehensive as it could be.

Last but not least, in order for us to create truly thriving communities, we will need abolition. But that's for another book.

Discussing Police Violence with Your Children

For families with children ages five to twelve years old

If or when your child has been exposed to the stories of contemporary police violence, there are several ways you could approach the conversation. Below is how we handle this topic with our children.

In 2017, Cobe attended the Montessori for Social Justice conference with me. During the conference, they created space to remember and celebrate Philando Castile. Philando Castile was an African American cafeteria supervisor in a Montessori school. His colleagues at the school said he was a great colleague and a role model to the students. He memorized the names of the five hundred children he served every day—along with their food allergies.[12]

On July 6, 2016, he was fatally shot during a traffic stop by a Minneapolis–St. Paul police officer. The traffic stop was streamed on Facebook Live by his partner (who was also in the passenger seat), where it went viral.

The conference had a table with art supplies, a candle, a bowl with water, flowers, a poem by my friend Betsy Romero, and a picture of Philando. People were invited to make artwork that would then be donated to the Castile family. Cobe saw the art supplies and immediately went over; he was drawn to create. I thought that this would be the best time to approach him about Philando.

I asked Cobe if he knew who Philando Castile was, and if so, what had happened to him. I pointed to the picture of Philando and asked, "Do you know who this is?"

Cobe: "Jesus?" [We had an image of Black Jesus in our home.]
Me: "No, his name is Philando Castile."
Cobe: "What happened to him? Did the cops kill him?"
Me: "Yes."

Cobe: "Why? What did he do?"
Me: "Nothing."

Up until this point, we hadn't had explicit conversations about police violence with Cobe; he was only four years old. But clearly, Cobe already drew the accurate conclusion: Black people are killed by the police. This is because the police are a constant presence in our neighborhood, and we hear the news stories and family stories about police violence toward Black and brown people often. As much as we wanted to protect Cobe by avoiding the conversation, I realized that the only way to better protect him was by discussing the realities of the situation.

Moving forward, as we approach conversations about police violence with our young children, here are some things I keep in mind:

1. **Do research:** Gather information about who the person was, not just what happened to them. So often, these killings result in viral videos desensitizing the world to the violence and brutality of Black bodies and reducing the victims to their last few minutes. Philando Castile, Sandra Bland, Breonna Taylor, and Tony McDade were people who had joy, love, and freedom in their lives. Find a photo of the person that you'd think they and their family would want you to share. Do research into the hobbies, favorite colors, family life, and community presence of the person; when you share with your child, you can tell a life story, not the story of the death. Prioritizing trauma and death won't lead to justice. Many times the victim's family has clear wishes or action items for us to follow, such as a GoFundMe or petition to support. Make a plan to follow through with these action items.

2. **Prepare a short story:** The goal here is to provide a clear, concise, and humanizing biography to present to your child. Young children's attention spans can be very short, so preparing a short story can help structure the conversation in a way that is efficient

and compassionate. Include the person's name, the information you found about the person, and how you will support the family.

3. **The conversation:** Tell your child you'd like to share a story with them to honor someone. Show your child the photo you found of the person and ask, "Do you know who this is?" If they correctly named them, ask, "What have you heard?" If they're unable to name them, share the person's name. From there, tell your prepared story to your child. Your children might become concerned about their safety or a loved one's safety. Reassure them they're safe right now. Follow up with, "I'm sharing this story with you because we want to keep people safe. We want the killings to stop. We'll need to take action to stop it." Every family is different, and each family will need to determine their course of action. For some, it means going to a protest, signing a petition, or participating in a boycott. Other families might commit to writing letters to representatives, calling their local police station to demand the release of body camera footage, and supporting local Bail Out organizations. Your advocacy will be based on your resources, location, age of children, and organizing skill level. We like to end the conversation by placing our hands on our hearts, taking a few deep breaths, and reminding ourselves that we still have breath in our lungs. We can and will advocate for change.

4. **What to do if there are questions:** Questions are a good thing; they mean the wheels are turning in your child's brain and that they're doing their best to understand. If your child asks a question that makes you uncomfortable, take a deep breath, move your body in a way that feels right to you, and lean into the tension. If you don't know the answer, you can always say, "I'm not sure. Details are coming out and I don't want to misinform you. Let's write it down and if I learn something new, I'll share it with you."

Together with your family, neighbors, and community members, you can create and affirm **values** that undermine oppression and re-envision safety and support for all community members. Recognize who's more at risk and collaborate to advocate and support them on their terms. Your community has the power to develop strategies and practices that can address issues and behavior within the community, and part of the solution will involve supporting fair housing, equitable quality education, and equitable access to human necessities for all of its members.

Keep in mind when introducing these topics and alternatives with your children that certain statements are not helpful when describing the history of policing and its disproportionate and discriminatory impacts, like "Don't worry, the police are our friends." That kind of statement just isn't true for all folks, and it's unhelpful when discussing discrimination.

Thinking about Our Neighbors without Houses

"Mom, why do all those people live under the bridge?" Shortly after moving to Houston, Texas, Carter started questioning housing accessibility. His concerns about his neighbors' living conditions grew, and he had several questions about the tent cities we drove past. If we use our antiracist lens, we can analyze what we learned about redlining and about the impact of policing to better understand houselessness. Many who are unhoused are denied kindness, consideration, and respect. Frequently, they're harshly judged by others, usually with an attitude of blame regarding their situation. Cartoonish stereotypes depicted in movies and on TV paint those who are unhoused traditionally as one-note addicts and dropouts, viewing these things as the sole reason why these folks are houseless, and also as reasons that they therefore don't deserve kindness and the human rights of shelter, food, water, and safety. This background information helped me respond to Carter's questions by utilizing my antiracist skills: "Housing is expensive, and Houston doesn't invest enough in affordable housing. Texas also doesn't mandate a living wage, so people have to make difficult choices." As antiracists, we're always looking for ways to system-blame instead of person-blame. System-blaming allows us to hold institutions and social services accountable to do better.

Stereotypes about addiction and dropouts within the houseless community are purposefully connected to perpetuated stereotypes of Black and brown people of the global majority. A 2018 study from the National Low Income Housing Coalition found that Black folks account for 12 percent of the population but disproportionately account for 43 percent of the homeless population.[13] If we truly understand the generations of systemic inequality caused by redlining, continued inequality caused by gentrification and wage gaps, and lack of societal support (financial, individual, and educational), we understand that houselessness is a failure of systems, not community members. With rising rents, lack of job security, and lack of generational wealth, many community members of color face more evictions than their white counterparts. Formerly incarcerated folks are also up to thirteen times more likely to experience houselessness, and due to policy, racism, poverty, unemployment, and flaws in the education system, African Americans are currently incarcerated across the country at about five times the rate of white people. In states such as Iowa, Minnesota, New Jersey, Vermont, and Wisconsin, the disparity is more than ten to one.[14] The goal is for children to understand houselessness is preventable and solvable through social programs, and that houselessness can also disproportionately affect some neighbors more than others.

As antiracists, we don't spend our time judging others for their circumstances; instead we judge the social services that have failed their particular communities. Besides, will any reason ever make it okay for people to be unhoused? No. Remember that as antiracists, we believe in collective care. We believe that all human beings deserve the right to shelter, food, water, and safety. We believe in blaming systems, not people. We believe in advocating for those that need our support against systemic injustices.

As always, be sure to discuss these topics with your children; don't ignore them. If they ask about houselessness, don't shy away from the conversation. Consistently model empathy and extend compassion to your community members. Provide opportunities for your children to understand the importance of recognizing the many facets of your community members' particular circumstances. Encourage your children to think of ways you both can contribute to community members who are unhoused, whether it's donating food, toys, money, or time. Make it clear that you support affordable housing initiatives and will vote to increase affordable housing in your neighborhood. This means voting to increase rental assistance programs, provide affordable home ownership programs, and provide home repair programs. For children seven and older, write letters to city and state officials demanding an increase in affordable housing, or speak at your local city council meetings. For more solutions, check out *Yes!* magazine's 2018 Affordable Housing Issue.

Loving Our Land

For communities to thrive, the land they inhabit must be cared for and considered. For communities to be antiracist, we must know the land we occupy is stolen and colonized, and its history has been rewritten.

Non-Indigenous and non-Native caregivers need to do some form of land acknowledgment with our children. A land acknowledgment is a prepared statement that recognizes and respects Indigenous and

Native people as the land's traditional stewards. It shows recognition of and respect for Aboriginal, Indigenous, and Native communities, their current presence, their history, and their forced removal/genocide, which is key to reconciliation. Land acknowledgments are powerful because they create and foster awareness and lay the groundwork for more informed action while also disrupting settler colonialism. America is stolen land, and there are many Indigenous communities that, through losing their land, lost not only their homes but also facets of their medicine, culture, and traditions.

Land acknowledgments don't just exist as a one-time event to address past genocide or forced removal: colonialism and white domination are ongoing and ever-present. These statements aren't just about the past but about the contemporary, too. Our children should build awareness of their participation in its perpetuation, and they can do so by doing regular land acknowledgments. Children as young as three years old can begin to learn the native names of plants, animals, and the land they occupy. Around five years old, we can introduce our children to Turtle Island maps.

You can encourage your child's school and classroom to partner with local Indigenous and Native communities so they can implement land acknowledgments as part of their day-to-day. In schools, children recite the pledge of allegiance to both the United States flag and, in some states, the state flag. Land acknowledgments can and should be incorporated into the classroom, since the land existed before the United States came to be and before statehood was created.

There will be an activity in the practice section that details steps you can take to create your own land acknowledgment with your child. Know that there's no real formula or set standard on structure, so doing the proper research and connecting to the Native and Indigenous communities in your area will be key to crafting a statement that feels sufficient, respectful, and honoring. Also know that a land acknowledgment isn't where things should end. You and your child can work to support Indigenous communities by redistributing funds and contacting local officials about policy, protection, and reconciliation. Lastly, co-conspirators work to redistribute native land back.

Land Acknowledgment

For families with children ages six and older

Research: You and your child can begin by learning the history of the land you're inhabiting and the Indigenous and Native peoples who originally lived there. There are several websites you can use to look up the territories, languages, and treaties of the land's history and the Indigenous peoples' histories. Native Land's interactive map[15] is a great resource that showcases these things, providing information to help you and your child unpack your land's history of colonialism and forced removal. As you learn about the people who live there, both past and present, do research about the tribe, the language, the culture, and their history. Together, you can write up an acknowledgment that includes this newfound knowledge. As your family begins their journey, use these markers to keep the conversation going:

- Start with one phrase: "This is Winnebago's land."
- Memorize the names of traditional stewards of the land and the languages spoken.
- A starting introduction paragraph for you and your six-year-old to draft together could look like:

  I live on the homelands of the Atakapa-Ishak people. The Atakapan people are a southeastern culture of Native American tribes who spoke Atakapa and historically lived along the Gulf of Mexico. They called themselves the Ishak, pronounced "ee-SHAK," which translates as "the People." There were two tribes within their Tribal Nation, "the Sunrise People" and "the Sunset People." Descendants still live, work, and play in Louisiana and Texas.

Connect: After researching, make an event of going out into the land with your child and truly connecting with it. Take a silent walk in a local park or canyon and sketch local flora and fauna together. Make a note of the flora and fauna in your home language, and in the Indigenous language.

Acknowledge and Reach Out: It's important to point children toward honoring and acknowledging the *contemporary* existence of their local Indigenous communities, as well. While many tribes have been wiped out, there are over five hundred tribes that are still here. Because of colonialism, forced resettlement, and separation of families, some Indigenous folks experienced an erasure of their culture, language, and traditions and an interruption in their parenting patterns, so in addition to honoring and acknowledging that past, we should support local Indigenous tribes.

This is where action can come into play:

1. **Build Authentic Relationships with Indigenous Communities**— Reach out to ask what you can do for your local Indigenous communities.
2. **Compensate and Donate to Indigenous People**—Instead of going hard on grocery shopping on Thanksgiving or having a spending spree during Black Friday, why not make annual donations and create volunteer traditions with your family?
3. **Constantly Acknowledge and Educate**—Doing a land acknowledgment once doesn't mean you don't need to do one ever again. By acknowledging the land and its history multiple times, you will help craft mindfulness and awareness for yourself and your child. Be sure to educate others and acknowledge the land around them, as well. The goal should always be to inspire action.

Community Schooling and Education: What Roles Do Schools Play in Perpetuating White Domination and Socialization?

Schools are ground zero for racism. They are not the apolitical, utopian places many imagine them to be. In 2018, Learning for Justice conducted a nationwide survey, in which they found that most hate and bias incidents witnessed by educators were not addressed by school leaders and nine out of ten administrators failed to denounce the bias.

Racial illiteracy is thriving, and schools can play a key part in teaching racial literacy to dismantle white domination. We can imagine how educators—when trusted and trained—can facilitate conversations about racism. Schools can be places where children can practice diagnosing the root causes of a problem, teaching them to create sustainable solutions. I can't think of a better way to educate a generation into becoming antiracist citizens.

However, the majority of schools in the United States shy away from conversations about racism, fearing backlash, lawsuits, reality, and change. Instead, schools continue to use textbooks that whitewash history, oversimplify movements, and victimize people of the global majority.

Remembering as an Act of Resistance

Carter once had a history assignment: *Write a letter to your cousin in England about life in Jamestown and how it's different from Plymouth in 1620.* Over dinner, he casually shared the details of his letter. Carter responded with the standard "put yourself in a white colonizer's shoes" and gave a vanilla answer to earn four out of four on the rubric. Afterward, I said, "Something in me isn't feeling right." I grabbed four sticky notes and started writing. In the following minutes, Carter and

I had processed together to identify the problems and create a solution using these questions:

- Who was erased during this assignment?
- Who was being centered or affirmed?
- What is this assignment assuming or promoting?
- Why was this assignment insensitive?

Below are Carter's responses:

Who felt affirmed?	Who was erased?
White children	People of the global majority
European descendants	Indigenous People
People who believe in colonization	Black People

What is the activity assuming or promoting?
You are European
Promoting colonization
Demoting people of the global majority

Why was this activity insensitive?
It is not actually talking about the whole truth, just white people's truth.

Moving forward, how can you respond differently?
I can represent and center Black, Indigenous, people of color in my responses.

Fortunately for Carter, we spent time using the work of the 1619 Project at home. Unfortunately for his classmates, this casual racism went unchecked.

Carter rewrote his response, sharing how life in Jamestown was different from Plymouth because Jamestown had over twenty enslaved Africans. Remembering our (people of the global majority's) stories, our history, and our experiences, he was able to center them as an act of resistance. Our roles are to help children think critically about the truths they're being presented, unpack the biases in the classroom, and when necessary, move to action. But this responsibility shouldn't only fall on Black children, one teacher, or one class; it needs to be everyone's responsibility.

How Can We Make Schools Safe for Children of All Races and Identities?

So much of this work is about advocating for yourself and your neighbors in the name of justice. In Part Two, we touched on dress codes, policies that disproportionately harm children of the global majority, trans and nonbinary youth, and girls. In addition to dress codes, there are more policies and practices school boards need to update and enact immediately, including their suicide prevention, holiday celebrations, bathroom policies, and community partnerships.

According to the National Institute of Mental Health Information Resource Center: "As of 2018, suicide became the second leading cause of death in Black children aged 10–14, and the third leading cause of death in Black adolescents aged 15–19. By combining data from 2001 to 2015, researchers were able to examine suicides among children ages 12 and younger and found that Black children were more likely to die by suicide than their White peers."[16] The Trevor Project created a Model School District Policy on Suicide Prevention, a document that outlines "model policies and best practices for school districts to follow to protect the health and safety of all students." As the Trevor Project notes, it's important that schools have policies in place to "prevent, assess the risk of, intervene, and respond to youth suicidal behavior. . . . Nevertheless, only 16 states require school districts to institute any suicide prevention policy."[17]

The ACLU notes that millions of students are in schools with law enforcement present, but no support staff available:

- 1.7 million students are in schools with police but no counselors
- 3 million students are in schools with police but no nurses
- 6 million students are in schools with police but no school psychologists
- 10 million students are in schools with police but no social workers
- 14 million students are in schools with police but no counselors, nurses, psychologists, or social workers

To make schools safer, we call for the defunding and removal of police in schools. According to the ACLU: "Given the clear benefits of investing in school mental health resources, it would make sense for school boards, school principals, and government leaders to be using every available resource to increase school-based health professionals. Yet that has not been the trend. Instead, funding for police in schools has been on the rise, while public schools face a critical shortage of teachers, counselors, nurses, psychologists, and social workers."

As Geo Maher notes in the subtitle of his book *A World Without Police*, strong communities make police obsolete. What we need in our schools instead of police officers are college counselors, full-time certified school nurses, and child therapists to handle ongoing grief, thoughts of suicide, substance use, pornography addictions, vaping, bullying, harassment, and racism. We need to invest in the arts and humanities. We need to prioritize children's growth and expression during a formative and difficult time. We also need to invite elders and community activists to be involved in our children's education, and we need to create group spaces (such as community gardens) that can help bring a more holistic approach to education.

How Can We Make Schools Affirming for Children of All Races and Identities?

Anti-bias and antiracism in school can be achieved through strategic planning, such as ongoing faculty and staff training, redesigning curriculum, updating human resource policies, and making space for student partnership.

Antiracist committees made up of students, staff, teachers, administrators, caregivers, and community members is also a way to start. As a committee, seek to change the current inequitable outcomes by making measurable and specific goals to achieve equity. Antiracist work will take a long-term commitment from you and your partners (co-teachers, assistants, administration, family groups, etc.) to successfully scale and communicate progress. Developing goals will require a constant examination of yourself to either continue a practice, reform a practice, or innovate a new one. We've invited fellow antiracist Tiffany Jewell to speak on her experience not only trying to change her children's school from within, but making a move to an antiracist school when all else failed.

Moving Beyond Peace

Our story is one of purposeful change. We firmly believed in the Montessori philosophy. The beautiful classrooms had natural materials, and the teachers were kind and talked to their students as if they were equals. We loved that our children learned how to care for themselves and their environment at the school. They gained confidence in their ability to trust themselves as learners. We loved the foundation it gave both of our children, but it wasn't enough. In our family we deeply value a community that upholds anti-bias, antiracist beliefs and practices. We value a community that always works for a more just and equitable way to teach and support all children. This is our story of finding our community.

I'm a Black-biracial, cisgender woman. My partner is a white cisgender man. Our children currently self-identify as white cisgender boys. Both children attended the local independent Montessori school where I worked as an educator. Our eldest (who's now nine years old) started on his second birthday, and our youngest (who's now five years old) started when he was sixteen months old. Both children enjoyed school and loved learning in an environment where they used didactic materials and had autonomy in their learning and well-being. Our eldest had several close friends from toddlerhood into first grade. The youngest always told us "everyone in my class is my friend."

Neither of our children stood out from their classmates. Both boys walk through the world with light skin and identify as white, and most of their classmates were white and from middle-class and upper-middle-class homes. All of their classroom teachers were white, the curriculum was Eurocentric, and the school placed an emphasis on peace and kindness without ever addressing justice. Their concept of peace was one that emphasized kindness and sameness. "We're all a family under one sky" was a song that was sung often. It didn't, however, feel that way. We weren't okay with our children not being explicitly taught about identity and justice. We wanted our children to engage in conversations about justice and resistance, but that wasn't happening. Our children were learning about the different parts of flowers, about European artists, geometric shapes, and how to care for their environment. Our oldest was learning about the history of racism and resistance and how to stand up, but that was because I was one of his teachers. Beyond my classroom, the work we wanted for our children just wasn't happening. Both of our children saw themselves reflected every day at that school. Yet still, so much was missing.

Additionally, as our children grew and our parenting became more conscious and purposeful, we were no longer okay with paying for a tuition-based school. We didn't want to redistribute our family funds to an independent institution where there are no classroom teachers of the global majority and the student population wasn't as racially and socioeconomically expansive as the community. We wanted to put our money and our resources of time and our energy into a more racially, ethnically, and socioeconomically diverse community—into *our* community.

In short: we were actively creating a community for our children and family that we did not truly believe in.

We didn't want our children to be surrounded and affirmed in their whiteness every day. Instead, we want them to grow in a community where they have friendships and relationships with children who are like them *and* who are different from them. We want our children to be able to make choices in who they seek out for friendships. We want them to have teachers who are people of the global majority, and we don't want them to be limited by the few white families able to pay for independent schooling. We're hoping to raise conscious children who understand that, when they walk through the world as white boys, people will make space for them, listen to them, and believe them. They will be validated and affirmed. They walk through this world with privilege and immunity, always. We hope to raise children who understand racism and oppression and the role they have in resisting and standing up against it. We strive to grow our family in a community that's racially and socioeconomically expansive, one where we can all hold authentic relationships with people in our community and be our full and whole selves.

I worked at the Montessori school for fifteen years and, in my classroom, I was able to do a lot. I was able to make and hold space for Black and Brown students. I was able to share the histories of the Great Law of Peace, the Black Panther Party, Malcolm X, Sojourner Truth, the Young Lords, and so many more. Students in my classroom were moved to be activists and stand up for racial, gender, and economic justice. They explored identity freely and grew as a community with purposeful intention. My classroom was an anomaly in that school. Despite the many initiatives I started or was a part of, despite the many articles and books I shared and the anti-bias antiracist trainings I brought to the school, very little changed.

My husband witnessed my growing frustration. He listened to me vent and dream. He noticed that the older our children became, the bigger my annoyance and anger grew. He reminded me we had the power of choice. We could enroll our children in other schools if we wanted to.

It was never our intention to have our children in private school. We both attended public elementary schools and I'm the product of pre-K through to twelfth-grade public school. Our children were independent school kids by default. Because I worked at the school (and it was therefore convenient), we got a tuition reduction. It was also the only school I knew a lot about. Because it felt safe for all of those reasons, we didn't even think of sending our kids elsewhere. We created this default for ourselves. We were raising children in a way that very much aligned with the Montessori philosophy and pedagogy instead of our own. We initially chose the school of comfort, familiarity, and ease.

But our school of comfort wasn't supporting the growth in our beliefs and values. It wasn't putting justice and equity at the center. It was, as many independent schools do, putting the wants of the full-paying families over everything else.

We chose to leave the school of comfort. All of the staff knew our children and our children knew them. They were a part of the kids' birth stories, their toileting journeys, and so much more. But it wasn't enough. It was limiting our children's ability to grow. While our children were being challenged academically, they weren't challenged to grow from discomfort because there was none. The school was creating a bubble for our children, and that was not okay with us. We couldn't wait for the school of comfort to become integrated, more "diverse," and equity focused. We can't change the environment, we can't change people; what we could change is ourselves. After our decision to make a change, we had multiple conversations with each other and with our oldest child about moving schools. (The youngest was two at the time and he was going to stay at the Montessori school through preschool.)

We were surprised at how ready our oldest child was for this move. We talked with him about it soon after he finished the History of Racism and Antiracism study in our classroom. We discussed the value in building relationships with all people in our community and not just the few white kids and their families he was with on a daily basis. He was more ready than we were for the transition and change. He was ready for this move from the school of comfort because this is the work we've been doing since before he was born. My husband and I have always been open and honest with each other and our children about what's happening in the world, about the way privilege and immunity take up space in our lives, and the ways we don't have to fall into the ease of white supremacy and its culture.

The research into figuring out in which school to enroll our oldest child (and the youngest once he came of age for kindergarten) started out before we realized it. One of the things about being a teacher in a private school is I had the ability to work with principals and special education teachers in the different public schools and districts where my students came from. I was able to "peek" into each school, see what they were like, and meet the folks who cared for the most vulnerable students. This previous access and knowledge helped tremendously.

My husband and I also looked up information about the

schools with a simple Google search of "_____ public school statistics." We were able to see the number of students in the schools, how many students receive free and reduced lunch, the student-teacher ratio, the general racial/ethnic makeup of the student population, and more (including test scores and academic proficiencies). Learning this information and my experiences of working with the SPED staff at many different public schools helped us to make an informed decision. We had the power of choice and we used that power to apply for a spot at the school in our district that had been centering the work of anti-bias education for twenty years. Our school of choice wasn't the one with the highest academic ratings, or the one with the lowest student-teacher ratio, it's the one where the teaching staff represented the student population. There, students saw adults who looked like them and could hear their home languages spoken. While most of the teachers were still white women, our children, their classmates, and their peers also had teachers who were Black, Latine/x, and Asian. It's a school where staff were not only familiar with the goals of anti-bias education but practiced them and implemented them into the curriculum. Black Lives Matter buttons were worn on the lanyards of staff members, a message received by students daily. This past year, amid the global pandemic, the school took on a community-wide antiracist commitment. The teachers and staff worked together to build out their curriculum to expand the children's exploration of identity, community, history, racism, and resistance from kindergarten through to fifth grade. Being a part of a school community where all of the adults were willing to embrace antiracism has been empowering for our oldest child. Our oldest knows the adults at home and the adults at school will stand up against racism and injustice, which helps him continue to grow into his antiracist self. Soon, my youngest will join him.

So much of our role as the caregivers of cisgender boys who

walk through the world presenting as white is to guide them in their growth. We are growing as a family. Our children are growing! Their growth isn't just physical, it's their continued understanding of who they are as individuals, family members, and community members. The boys' growth includes their understanding of their many different identities (both social and personal) and knowing how they hold privilege and immunity because of the color of their skin. Our children are growing up during a time when the death of a Black person (regardless of their age or gender) no longer elicits shock. Our children know about Tamir Rice and George Floyd; they know about Philando Castile and Sandra Bland. They're learning how to take action and resist racial injustice. They know that resting on the laurels of kindness is not enough. We want our children to be in a community that goes beyond the passivity of kindness.

—Tiffany Jewell

Below are questions **caregivers raising children of the global majority** can ask their school administrators and teachers:

1. Could you tell me about the racial makeup of the class?
2. Can you share how the books and curriculum represent Black, Indigenous, Asian, and other ethnicities?
3. Will group identities be explicitly acknowledged and celebrated in a developmentally appropriate way? How do you introduce heavy topics such as slavery to the students? How do you change the language to make the content more developmentally appropriate for their age?
4. How have you noticed pre-prejudice and racism showing up in the classroom? How will I be notified if my child experiences pre-prejudice or racism? And how will I be notified if my child is committing pre-prejudice?
5. What groups or programs are available to learn more about antiracism and inclusion?
6. Does the school offer racial affinity groups?
7. I'm concerned about the school's academic expectations and discipline when it comes to (insert racialized identity) children. What is your classroom management or behavior plan? How are you taking into consideration teacher bias?
8. We're raising antiracist children to notice and interrupt racism when they see it. How will this be received?
9. Is there a particular framework you're using to teach your students about racial justice or social justice?
10. In your classroom, which holidays, celebrations, and social justice movements are taught?
11. Will my children see themselves represented in the faculty and staff at this school?

For caregivers raising white children, you can and should still ask questions 1–10. Additionally, ask the following questions:

1. How will you support our children in understanding the privilege and immunity that comes with their racialized identity?
2. How will you ensure ALL students are equipped to stand up and speak out against injustice—*especially* white students and those who fit into the dominant culture of society?
3. Is the school currently assessing and addressing the education debt owed to students of the global majority? What is being done to enact change?

—Tiffany Jewell and Britt Hawthorne

> Education debt describes the compounded result of the generational defunding and divestment of schools of color, fewer present financial resources, and other harm and lack of support directed at students of color. The term was coined by Gloria Ladson-Billings.

Conversations with Your Child's Teacher About Race

We have to expect schools will be affirming spaces for every child and we must work with our local school to ensure it's happening. This means asking the right questions, accepting the present reality, and working toward future liberation.

I've invited my friends Lorena and Roberto Germán to share how their children experienced texturism (which is a form of racism) in their school and how they chose to confront it.

Black Hair & the Sandbox

We're Lorena and Roberto. We're Dominican, and we identify racially as Black. Our children were all born in the United States and are being raised to know about, and relate to, their Dominican identity in addition to their American culture. This has been quite a journey, one with moments of laughter and frustration.

Our children all have beautiful curly hair. It curls and waves and glistens when water falls on it. Their hair is strong-willed and opinionated, like them. We know that American society doesn't see the brilliance in their hair or their beauty, so we work diligently to build up their self-love, hair included.

When our daughter Analiz was in pre-kindergarten, the sandbox and experiences with sand became a source of stress. Her 4a hair type is a marvel to behold. It shapes and morphs into so many beautiful styles. It's thick, wild, and bold, like her energy. It's a great representation of her inner spunk. It also doesn't fit white standards of beauty, and so to prepare her for what will be a challenging journey of self-esteem, we protected her hair experiences from an early age.

One day, after playing in the sandbox, she came home with sand all over her hair. It was in between the strands, on her scalp . . . all over. At bath time we tried to get it out. It was difficult, to say the least. It was forty-five minutes of crying, poking, and pulling back and forth. It was the very thing we feared: a negative experience related to her hair. We didn't want hair washing to yield the idea that her hair was bad, difficult, or a problem, or produce any other negative connotation. We told Analiz that "the issue is not your hair. It's the sand."

It happened several other times. Lorena was frustrated that Analiz's teachers didn't understand how this was an issue and weren't protecting her hair. Analiz's teachers needed to provide her more care, consideration, and protection in these play spaces than her classmates with straight hair. Together, we communicated with them; we emailed her school an explanation and invited them to have a problem-solving conversation with us. After talking, it was clear that she loved the sandbox. The sensory experience was something she enjoyed, and being in there was a sweet moment each day that she looked forward to. We didn't want her hair to be the reason she couldn't play. After some brainstorming, we agreed to send her hair bonnet with her. Now with the bonnet, there was playtime in the sandbox and freedom from sand in her hair.

—Lorena and Roberto Germán

Problem-Solving with Your Children's Teachers

For parents and caregivers

This practice was written by Lorena and Roberto Germán for families of the global majority needing to have a critical conversation with your children's teachers, but this could also extend to your children's coaches, mentors, spiritual leaders, camp counselors, and other adults who play a key role in shaping your child's identity.

Start with Your Child

Make sure your child fully understands what the issue is and that you're ready to take action to help them. It's important that they know they're not the problem. Point out that you want to make sure they're cared for and that their health, happiness, and safety are a priority.

1. Communicate with Your Parenting Partners

Talk about the issue, the potential outcomes, and your own past experiences. Together, develop expectations for the meeting with the teacher(s). Check on each other to make sure this isn't triggering older pains. Sometimes what happens to our children hints at our own past experiences and we react from a place of pain and trauma. Take deep breaths and focus on problem-solving. You're in this together.

2. Communicate with the Teachers

Face-to-face is always best (when possible) to ensure that teachers understand how important your issue is—and how much is at stake. The teachers might need help in understanding the problem and using antiracist skills to solve it. Kindness, patience, and firmness are the way to go here. You are the expert in your child's life; trust yourself. You know what's best.

3. Develop a Strategy

Collaborate to identify ways to help the child have agency in the situation. What are ways you can all come together to support the child? What is possible and feasible?

—Lorena and Roberto Germán

Parent-Teacher Organizations

Parent-Teacher Organizations (PTOs) have power in schools. They can play a pivotal role in the school's progress and impact, from community building to fundraising. Holding a PTO leadership role is exhausting but enjoyable work. Many folks end up volunteering because no one else steps up to do the job and someone needs to. Other folks gravitate toward the PTO due to the increase in power and influence. To support antiracist efforts, consider joining your child's school PTO. PTO leadership is privy to school information before anyone else and with this knowledge comes power, influence, and action. From the inside, you can work with PTO leadership (and sometimes against it) to make PTOs more inclusive, forward-thinking, and antiracist. Here are some examples of incremental changes you can suggest to fellow PTO members:

1. **Check in with the school community.** Survey families each year to find out how they would like to engage with the school—when can they come? What events would they like to attend? What skills are they able to contribute?

2. **Make time for introductions at PTO meetings.** Name tags with the caregiver's name/pronouns help people get to know each other. It's a nice touch to add the child's name, grade level, and teacher, too.

3. **Make events affordable and accessible.** PTOs can create family directories, cookbooks, yearbooks, and other community-building activities that are lower cost. For ticketing events, instead of a required price, offer a suggested price or a sliding scale.

4. **Build community connections.** If your school is a magnet school, make a commitment to have gatherings around the city. Utilize public playgrounds, community centers, and libraries for informal gatherings. PTOs within the same school district can work together

to cohost events. They can plan school field trips and teacher professional development opportunities.

5. **Make PTO membership financially inclusive.** PTO membership shouldn't be limited to those who can afford a fee or have important connections. All parents can and should have the right to make positive change and build connections for their children.

6. **Share funds equitably.** PTOs within the same school district can pool funds into one large, centralized pot with the mission of equitable redistribution. Doing this centers economically disadvantaged schools and supports the mission of public school.

Practices

Nurturing Solidarity

For parents and caregivers

1. When you were young, who were the adults in your life that helped nurture you? What role(s) did they play in shaping you to become antiracist? _____

   _____

2. Who are your parenting partners now? How are they supporting you and your children in becoming antiracist? _____

   _____

3. For families of color: Who (if any) are the white adults in your child's life, and how are they working in solidarity with you? _____

   _____

4. For white families: Who (if any) are the adults of color in your child's life? How are you working to mitigate harm? _____

   _____

5. What are you doing to sustain your cross-racial friendships? _____

   _____

How Diverse Is Your Universe?

For parents and caregivers

Complete the following questions to truly understand just how diverse your universe is.

Your Universe	Racialized Identity
I am:	
My partner is:	
My child(ren) is/are	
My children's peers are:	
The teachers at my children's school are predominantly:	
The administrators at my children's school are predominantly:	
The school's staff at my children's school are predominantly:	
Most of my children's close friends are predominantly:	
Most of my close friends are predominantly:	
Most of my neighbors are predominantly:	
People who regularly visit my home are predominantly:	

Now, reflect on the following:

I felt . . .
I found . . .
I fear . . .

Noticing

For families with children of all ages

Parenting partners: Notice who you wave to, hold the door open for, and smile at, notice who you engage in conversation with and how, and notice your body language and comfort or discomfort. We're constantly sending subtle messages to our children with our actions. Be mindful of what you're modeling for your children.

For families with children three to six years old, noticing is a powerful, low-risk tool to build awareness and offer opportunities for conversation. Just by noticing, we are resisting ignorance and choosing to be in reality. Together, with your child:

- Name the types of places you see around town: _____
  _____

- Name the languages you hear and experience: _____
  _____

- Who's helpful in your neighborhood? Who are they helpful to? ____
  _____

- What's missing from your neighborhood? _____
  _____

For families with children age seven and older, continue to notice, but now be race-conscious with your noticing. Discuss why representation in your community is either vast or limited. Brainstorm ways diversity could have been achieved: advertising, marketing, social media fliers, scholarships, transportation, etc. Then follow up with organizers, leaders, and coaches to share your ideas.

Taking Action

For families with children ages seven and older

The goal of this exercise is for you and your children to brainstorm and research actions to take toward inclusive policy change and community care.

We live in: _____

(city/town)

Parenting partners: What are current issues related to health-care access, transportation access, and green spaces in your community directly related to your children's lives and family's life?

_____

_____

_____

_____

_____

Next, research and list the resources available to support your antiracist work related to the social issue in your neighborhood:

_____

_____

_____

_____

_____

Below is an example of how to address housing with your children, but please use this blueprint to address any social issues directly impacting your community.

Together as a family, respond to the following:

1. What are my beliefs about housing and who has the right to safe housing? _____

_____

2. What do I know about the cost of housing in my area? _____

   _____

3. Who lives in my neighborhood? _____

   _____

4. Who doesn't live in my neighborhood? _____

   _____

5. Are there local policies or programs dedicated to creating and pre-serving affordable housing? _____

   _____

6. Do I know of affordable housing near me/in my neighborhood? ___

   _____

If you're unsure where to start the conversation, think about: Black, Indigenous, Latine/x, Asian, people of the global majority, immigrants, people without houses, etc. Do you and your family notice any inequities/patterns? Discuss your findings and move to action to address these inequities as antiracist community members.

We hope that this part of the book has given you and your child tools to use toward becoming more conscious citizens who advocate for better, more equitable communities. We hope you've found tools that will help encourage your child to have authentic, accountable relationships, and that help you build a home based on trust, honesty, and accountability.

As always, keep in mind that these lessons aren't all-encompassing or the end-all-be-all. These are foundational topics and exercises to help you *begin* your journey. Keep growing and learning together to work toward liberation.

conclusion

White domination continues to spread because we have not taken aggressive action to dismantle it. We leave you with the tools to practice antiracism in your home, raise antiracist children, and build thriving inclusive communities. While others are busy complicating the history of racism, weighed down by their to-be-read lists, white domination is busy growing. It's our hope that folks invest the same energy they use for learning about the past toward changing the future for the better. Destroying white domination will take work, far more work than a three-point plan, a book club, or a social media hashtag. With this knowledge, we understand that dedication, commitment, and fearlessness are required. As we move to action, we know that mistakes belong and will occur. It's not about avoiding mistakes, it's about moving through them to reach liberation. There are thousands of families reading this book and doing the work right along with you. Allow this book to connect you with those families seeking liberation and love. Every time you revisit the practices, your family will deepen their understanding, become more confident, and move forward in your community and the world at large in a more informed way.

We're always learning, unlearning, relearning, and adjusting. As long as you and the children in your lives commit to holding one another accountable with love, compassion, and honesty, progress will be achieved. These lessons will be a key part of your child's growth; they'll help the children in your life be able to craft an equitable, liberated world. This book is only the beginning; the rest is up to you.

We're rooting for you,

Britt and Tasha

further resources for parents

This book is just one of the texts that can help you work toward self-awareness and liberation. Below is a selection of books and media we recommend diving into if you haven't already.

Resources for Part One: Deepening Our Understandings
Between the World and Me, by Ta-Nehisi Coates
The New Jim Crow, by Michelle Alexander
Me and White Supremacy, by Layla F. Saad
Stamped from the Beginning: The Definitive History of Racist Ideas in America, by Ibram X. Kendi
So You Want to Talk About Race, by Ijeoma Oluo
The *Raising Equity Podcast*
We Live for the We: The Political Power of Black Motherhood, by Dani McClain

Resources for Part Two: Healthy Bodies
The Body Is Not an Apology, by Sonya Renee Taylor
Disability Visibility: First-Person Stories from the Twenty-First Century, by Alice Wong
My Grandmother's Hands, by Resmaa Menakem
Why Are All the Black Kids Sitting Together in the Cafeteria? And Other Conversations about Race, by Beverly Daniel Tatum

Resources for Part Three: Radical Minds
Hood Feminism, by Mikki Kendall
How to Be an Antiracist, by Ibram X. Kendi
Permission to Come Home: Reclaiming Mental Health as Asian Americans, by Jenny Wang
White Supremacy Culture (http://www.whitesupremacyculture.info/about .html), by Tema Okun

The Body Keeps the Score: Brain, Mind, and Body in the Healing of Trauma, by Bessel van der Kolk

The *Queer Kid Stuff* YouTube channel (https://www.youtube.com/c/queer kidstuff)

Resources for Part Four: Conscious Consumption
The Afrominimalist's Guide to Living with Less, by Christine Platt
Consumed: The Need for Collective Change: Colonialism, Climate Change, and Consumerism, by Aja Barber
Decolonizing Wealth: Indigenous Wisdom to Heal Divides and Restore Balance, by Edgar Villanueva
Little Koto's Closet blog (https://littlekotoscloset.wixsite.com/mysite/blog)
Indigenous Cheerleader (www.indigenouscheerleader.com)

Resources for Part Five: Thriving Communities
A Promise and a Way of Life: White Antiracist Activism, by Becky Thompson
The Anti Racist Teacher: Reading Instruction Workbook, by Lorena Germán
Becoming Abolitionists: Police, Protests, and the Pursuit of Freedom, by Derecka Purnell
The Color of Law: A Forgotten History of How Our Government Segregated America, by Richard Rothstein
Just Mercy, by Bryan Stevenson
Policing the Black Man, by Angela J. Davis, Bryan Stevenson, Marc Mauer, Bruce Western, and Jeremy Travis
The *Pod Save the People* podcast

Further Reading for Kids

This book is just one of many texts the children in your lives can benefit from. Below is a list of books for you and the children in your life to read and enjoy.

Books for children birth to six years old
I Love My Family, by Laura Galvin Gates
Little Faces: Smiley Faces, by Claire Everett
Please, Baby, Please, by Spike Lee
A Is for Activist, by Innosanto Nagara
Don't Touch My Hair! by Sharee Miller
Hair Love, by Matthew A. Cherry, illustrated by Vashti Harrison
We're Different, We're the Same, by Bobbi Kates and Sesame Street, illustrated by Joe Mathieu
You Hold Me Up, by Monique Gray Smith

Different Differenter: An Activity Book about Skin Color, by Jyoti Gupta, illustrated by Tarannum Pasricha
The Proudest Blue: A Story of Hijab and Family, by Ibtihaj Muhammad and S. K. Ali, illustrated by Hatem Aly
All Are Welcome, by Alexandra Penfold, illustrated by Suzanne Kaufman
Our Skin: A First Conversation about Race, by Jessica Ralli, Megan Madison, et al.
Being You: A First Conversation about Gender, by Megan Madison, Jessica Ralli, et al.

Books for children seven to twelve years old
Bodies Are Cool, by Tyler Feder
We Are Still Here! by Traci Sorrell, illustrated by Frane Lessac
We Are Water Protectors, by Carole Lindstrom, illustrated by Michaela Goade
Suki's Kimono, by Chieri Uegaki
Eyes That Kiss in the Corners, by Joanna Ho, illustrated by Dung Ho
The Antiracist Kid: A Book About Identity, Justice, and Activism, by Tiffany Jewell, illustrated by Nicole Miles
Flying Lessons & Other Stories, by Ellen Oh
A Place Where Sunflowers Grow, by Amy Lee-Tai
Not My Idea: A Book About Whiteness, by Anastasia Higginbotham
Where Are You From? by Yamile Saied Méndez, illustrated by Jaime Kim (Spanish edition titled *¿De Dónde Eres?*)
The Name Jar, by Yangsook Choi
The Invitation, by Jennifer Phillips, illustrated by Ruthie Lafond (accessible for free on Literacy Cloud)
Oh, the Things We're For!, by Innosanto Nagara
Yä's Backyard Jungle, by H'Abigail Mlo, illustrated by Jesse White (accessible for free on Literacy Cloud)
IntersectionAllies: We Make Room for All, by Chelsea Johnson and Latoya Council, illustrated by Ashley Seil Smith
Healer of the Water Monster, by Brian Young
What Are Your Words: A Book About Pronouns, by Katherine Locke, illustrated by Anne Passchier

Books for children thirteen to eighteen years old
This Book Is Anti-Racist, by Tiffany Jewell
Just Mercy (Adapted for Young Adults): A True Story of the Fight for Justice, by Bryan Stevenson
An Indigenous Peoples' History of the United States for Young People, adapted by

Debbie Reese (Nambé Owingeh) and Jean Mendoza from the adult book by Roxanne Dunbar-Ortiz

With the Fire on High, by Elizabeth Acevedo

Orleans, by Sherri L. Smith

Race to Incarcerate: A Graphic Retelling, by Sabrina Jones and Marc Mauer

Cemetery Boys, by Aiden Thomas

All Boys Aren't Blue: A Memoir-Manifesto, by George M. Johnson

King of the Dragonflies, by Kacen Callender

Indivisible, by Daniel Aleman

They Called Us Enemy, by George Takei, Justin Eisinger, and Steve Scott

A Very Large Expanse of Sea, by Tahereh Mafi

The Rebellious Life of Mrs. Rosa Parks: Young Readers Edition, by Jeanne Theoharis and Brandy Colbert

contributors

Dr. Kira Banks (she/her) is a thought leader on antiracism, professor, and mother of two brilliant children who are teaching her more than she ever learned in school. Read about her work and check out her podcast *Raising Equity* at kirabanks.com.

Dr. Nicole Evans (she/her) is an educator and former school leader who lives in St. Louis, Missouri. She serves as the director of leadership and coaching at Embracing Equity, where she walks shoulder to shoulder with organizations and their leaders to create transformative change. Dr. Evans enjoys working to create racial equity for all.

Maribel Gonzalez (she/her) is an Indigenous Xicana educator. Antonio Manuel Castillo Gonzalez is an Indigenous Tejano artist. They are both the parents of Aztlaneci and Temixcalli, who are being raised to value and connect to their mother, the land, through consistent ceremonial practice.

Katie Kitchens (they/them) is a queer, white, Jewish educator who has worked in Montessori environments for the past decade as an instructional coach, teacher trainer, and primary and elementary guide. Currently, Katie is pursuing a PhD in educational studies, researching racial identity development in young white children.

Kerry LiBrando (she/her) is a Montessori Secondary–trained teacher who has spent most of her teaching career in majority white schools. She and her partner are cultivating an antiracist home by unlearning together while raising a powerful four-year-old and a new babe.

Trisha Moquino (she/her) is raising her sixteen-year-old and thirteen-year-old in their Tribal Nations of Kewa and Cochiti in New Mexico. Trisha is also a member of the Ohkay Ohwingeh Tribal Nation. She is the cofounder, education director, and elementary Keres speaking guide at Keres Children's Learning Center. She and her husband are raising their two teenage daughters to know their Keres language and cultural ways of being.

Lorena (she/her) and Roberto (he/him) Germán are Dominican American educators raising three bilingual and bicultural children. They're cofounders of Multicultural Classroom, authors, and speakers.

Joemy Ito-Gates (she/her) is a multiracial Japanese American mother, public educator, and Dharma School teacher. She is raising her bilingual Black, Japanese, Filipino, and white child with her loving husband on unceded Ohlone land. Joemy also volunteers with a Japanese American activist organization called Japanese American Families for Justice.

Amelia Allen Sherwood (she/her) is the dreamer of Sankofa Learning Center, an African-Centered Montessori learning center. She is raising Shiloh Brave and Nesta Tafari to be free, curious children. She lives on Quinnipiac land, but you may know it as New Haven, Connecticut.

Tiffany Jewell (she/her) is a Black biracial author educator. Her partner is a white computer programmer. Both of their children currently self-identify as white cisgender boys. They all currently live in a predominantly white city in New England. Tiffany and her partner are raising their children to actively resist white supremacy culture.

Christine Platt (she/her) is an advocate for policy reform and a beloved author who utilizes storytelling as a tool for social change. She holds a BA in Africana studies, an MA in African American studies, and a JD in general law. Christine has written over two dozen literary works for people of all ages. Her most recent book, *The Afrominimalist's Guide to Living with Less*, is a radical reenvisioning of minimalism that focuses on authenticity over aesthetics.

Dr. Saira Siddiqui (she/her) is a Muslim American whose people originate from the Indian subcontinent. She is a teacher turned writer who helps children and adults think more critically and inclusively. She chronicles her experiences unschooling her own children and raising global citizens in her blog, *Confessions of a Muslim Mom*.

Aja Barber (she/they) is a writer and sustainability consultant based in the UK. Aja's work centers around the fashion industry and its intersections with race, feminism, privilege, and inequality. Her debut book, *Consumed: The Need for Collective Change: Colonialism, Climate Change, and Consumerism*, is a call to action for people everywhere.

Andy Lulka (she/any) is a mixed-ethnicity Jewish immigrant to Canada from Mexico, and a nonbinary single parent of an interfaith child. Holding an MEd in Integrative Montessori Learning, Andy loves exploring the interplay between liminality, identity, belonging, communication, and education with learning communities of all ages.

acknowledgments

We acknowledge with deep gratitude the activists, ancestors, theorists, advocates, and dreamers who came before us and whose efforts, impacts, and contributions we build upon daily. We acknowledge with deep gratitude the parents, teachers, mentors, and caregivers who influenced the way we think about raising the next generation for the better. Thank you to our community of antiracist individuals who offered their insights, experiences, hopes, and practices to this book.

Britt would like to thank: First and foremost, my grandparents, the Paschals and the Hales, for your nurturing wisdom and unconditional love. My parents, for being my very first teachers, who instilled a love of learning and antiracist values. My beloved husband, Shayne, for your constant encouragement and support. Carter and Cobe, thank you for listening and learning with me, for sharing your stories with our readers, and for choosing the path less traveled. A special thank-you to Christine Platt for gifting me the opportunity to become an author. Tasha, my coauthor and friend, my deepest gratitude for your loving words and honest feedback. To my friends for the impromptu playdates, homemade dinners, kind messages, and gifts that sustained my family through the writing process. Monica Earnshaw, who was with me all along, rooting for me, and helping me to take care of myself. To all of the readers and doers, thank you, I love you. And last but certainly not least, I acknowledge myself for writing this book, for facing my fears, and for my relentless advocating.

Tasha would like to thank: To my friends and family who support me in my goals and my personal growth: thank you. In particular, I offer my deepest love and my profound gratitude to my father, Ari, David, Sahand, Niel, Summer, Ali, and Sherry, each of whom supported me in one form or another on a weekly basis (sometimes even daily). To my own beautiful, diverse network of learners, teachers, and activists for guiding me, holding me accountable, and encouraging me to keep learning. To the Bennington Writing Seminars for providing a beloved community. To Lyra for the comfort given during difficult days. Last but not least, thank you to Britt for being generous, patient, welcoming, and affirming. Thank you for choosing me to partner with you on this journey, first as an editor, then as a cowriter. Thank you to Shayne, Carter, and Cobe for sharing Britt with me, as well as your stories and your kindness.

notes

Introduction

1. Nick Morrison, "Black Students 'Face Racial Bias' in School Discipline," *Forbes*, April 5, 2019.
2. Sam Weber and Connie Kargbo, "Black Families Increasingly Choose to Homeschool Kids," PBS, April 22, 2018, https://www.pbs.org/newshour /show/black-families-increasingly-choose-to-homeschool-kids.

Part One: Deepening Our Understandings

1. Lindsey Craig, "Racial Bias May Begin in Babies at Six Months, U of T Research Reveals," U of T News, April 11, 2017, https://www.utoronto.ca /news/racial-bias-may-begin-babies-six-months-u-t-research-reveals.
2. Nolan L. Cabrera, "White Immunity: Working Through Some of the Pedagogical Pitfalls of 'Privilege,'" *Journal Committed to Social Change on Race and Ethnicity* 3, no. 1 (2017): 82.
3. Pirkei Avot 2:16.
4. David J. Kelly et al., "Three-Month-Olds, but Not Newborns, Prefer Own-Race Faces," *Developmental Science* 8, no. 6 (November 2005): F31–F36.
5. "Culture," Britannica Kids, accessed August 16, 2021.
6. Alicia Elliott, "Why Are Parents So Defensive about Play Teepees?" *Today's Parent*, November 28, 2017.

Part Two: Healthy Bodies

1. Alice Walker, *In Search of Our Mothers' Gardens: Womanist Prose* (San Diego: Harcourt Brace Jovanovich, January 1, 1983).
2. Margaret Hunter, *The Persistent Problem of Colorism: Skin Tone, Status, and Inequality* (Hoboken, NJ: Blackwell Publishing, 2007).
3. Chanté Griffin, "How Natural Black Hair at Work Became a Civil Rights

Issue," JSTOR Daily, July 3, 2019, https://daily.jstor.org/how-natural
-black-hair-at-work-became-a-civil-rights-issue/.

4. "Skin," *National Geographic*, January 18, 2017, https://www.nationalgeo
graphic.com/science/article/skin-1.

5. Kayla Lattimore, "When Black Hair Violates the Dress Code," NPR,
July 17, 2017, https://www.npr.org/sections/ed/2017/07/17/534448313
/when-black-hair-violates-the-dress-code.

6. Chloe Latham Sikes, "Racial and Gender Disparities in Dress Code Discipline Point to Need for New Approaches in Schools," Intercultural Development Research Association, February 2020, https://www.idra.org
/resource-center/racial-and-gender-disparities-in-dress-code-discipline
-point-to-need-for-new-approaches-in-schools/.

7. "Student Dress Policy No. 3224," Seattle School Board, July 10, 2019.

8. Ibid.

9. "Gender Identity," University of South Dakota, accessed August 16, 2021.

10. "Species," Merriam-Webster.com, accessed August 17, 2021.

Part Three: Radical Minds

1. Ijeoma Oluo, *So You Want to Talk about Race* (New York: Seal Press, 2020),
28.

2. David T. Wellman, *Portraits of White Racism* (Cambridge, MA: Cambridge
University Press, 1994).

3. Tema Okun, "White Supremacy Culture," https://www.dismantlingra
cism.org/white-supremacy-culture.html.

4. Ibid.

5. Ibid.

6. Eugene L. Meyer, "Five Black Men Raided Harpers Ferry with John Brown.
They've Been Forgotten," *Washington Post*, October 13, 2019, https://
www.washingtonpost.com/history/2019/10/13/five-black-men-raided
-harpers -ferry-with-john-brown-theyve-been-forgotten/.

7. "White Antiracism in U.S. History," Cross Cultural Solidarity History
Project, accessed May 10, 2021, https://crossculturalsolidarity.com/white
-antiracism-in-u-s-history/.

8. Dr. Dafna Lemish and Dr. Colleen Russo Johnson, "The Landscape of
Children's Television in the US & Canada," Center for Scholars & Storytellers, April 2019.

Part Four: Conscious Consumption

1. "Ethical Consumerism," *Encyclopedia Britannica*, accessed August 16,
2021.

2. Homepage, Good on You, https://goodonyou.eco.

3. Homepage, Slow Factory Foundation, https://slowfactory.earth.
4. Homepage, Intersectional Environmentalist, http://intersectionalenviron mentalist.com.
5. "Where to Buy Fair Trade Chocolate," Fair Trade Certified, accessed August 16, 2021, https://www.fairtradecertified.org/shopping-guides/fair -trade-chocolate.
6. Pedro Nicolaci da Costa, "The Covid-19 Crisis Has Wiped Out Nearly Half of Black Small Businesses," *Forbes*, August 10, 2020, https://www .forbes.com/sites/pedrodacosta/2020/08/10/the-covid-19-crisis-has -wiped-out-nearly-half-of-black-small-businesses/?sh=7c3ef2184310.
7. Aaron Morrison, "100 Years After Tulsa Race Massacre, the Damage Remains," Associated Press, May 25, 2021, https://apnews.com/ar ticle/tulsa-race-massacre-1921-100-years-later-3bc13e842c31054a90b 6d1c81db9d70c.
8. Patrick J. Kiger, "Minimum Wage in America: A Timeline," History.com, October 18, 2019.
9. Emma Specter, "'Emotional Labor' Is Not What You Think It Is," *Vogue*, November 20, 2019, https://www.vogue.com/article/what-is-emotional -labor.
10. Kamala Harris, "Who Else Keeps Their Spices in Taster's CHOICE Jars? Turns Out @MindyKaling and I Have More in Common than We Initially Thought. WATCH: HTTPS://T.CO/HQQL2OYB3D PIC.TWITTER .COM/9DGQUJKEZF," Twitter, November 26, 2019.
11. Norberto Briceño, "This Damn Cookie Tin," BuzzFeed, August 31, 2020.
12. "Ethane Cracker Plants: What Are They?" Climate Reality Project, October 23, 2018, https://www.climaterealityproject.org/blog/ethane-cracker -plants-what-are-they.
13. Ayana Byrd, "STUDY: Pennsylvania's Communities of Color in More Danger from Health Consequences of Fracking," Colorlines, June 20, 2018, https://www.colorlines.com/articles/study-pennsylvanias-communi ties-color-more-danger-health-consequences-fracking; and Kelly Coles, "Fracking Disproportionately Affects Communities of Color in Texas, Study Shows, *Texas Monthly*, November 17, 2017, https://www.texas monthly.com/news-politics/fracking-disproportionately-affects-communi ties-color-texas-study-shows/.
14. Ana Isabel Baptista and Adrienne Perovich, "U.S. Municipal Solid Waste Incinerators: An Industry in Decline," Tishman Environment and Design Center at The New School, May 2019.
15. Linda Rodriguez and Vincent Ha, "Commentary: The Plastics Industry Continues to Treat Black and Brown Lives as Disposable," *San Diego Union-Tribune*, July 16, 2020, https://www.sandiegouniontribune.com

/opinion/commentary/story/2020-07-16/health-risks-plastic-industry
-commentary.

16. "Brands," 15 Percent Pledge, accessed August 16, 2021.

Part Five: Thriving Communities

1. "Act, Strategies, Caucus and Affinity Groups," Racial Equity Tools, accessed August 16, 2021, https://www.racialequitytools.org/resources/act/strategies/caucus-and-affinity-groups.

2. Barbara J. Love, "Developing a Liberatory Consciousness," Oregon State University, https://app.uhds.oregonstate.edu/intranet/files/Public/CRF%20Class/Week%203/Developing%20a%20Liberatory%20Consciousness%20-%20Barbara%20Love.pdf.

3. Suniya S. Luthar, Jacob A. Burack, Dante Cicchetti, and John R. Weisz, eds., *Developmental Psychopathology: Perspectives on Adjustment, Risk, and Disorder* (New York: Cambridge University Press, 1997).

4. Po Bronson and Ashley Merryman, "Even Babies Discriminate: A Nurture-Shock Excerpt," *Newsweek*, September 4, 2009, https://www.newsweek.com/even-babies-discriminate-nurtureshock-excerpt-79233.

5. "Appendix A: For Students," Learning for Justice, accessed August 16, 2021, https://www.learningforjustice.org/magazine/publications/speak-up-at-school/appendices/appendix-a-for-students.

6. Brittany Wong, "Why We Need More Close Interracial Friendships (And Why We're Bad at Them)," *HuffPost*, September 4, 2020, https://www.huffpost.com/entry/close-interaacial-friendships_l_5f5122c8c5b6946f3eaed704.

7. Angela Rowen, "Minority Communities Need More Parks, Report Says," *Berkeley Daily Planet*, November 13, 2007, https://www.berkeleydailyplanet.com/issue/2007-11-13/article/28458.

8. Victoria W. Wolcott, "The Forgotten History of Segregated Swimming Pools and Amusement Parks," *Conversation*, July 9, 2019, https://theconversation.com/the-forgotten-history-of-segregated-swimming-pools-and-amusement-parks-119586.

9. Fred Rogers, *The World According to Mister Rogers: Important Things to Remember* (New York: Hachette Books, 2019).

10. "About Wee The People," Wee The People, https://www.weethepeopleboston.org/about.

11. Ryan Gabrielson, Eric Sagara, and Ryann Grochowski Jones, "Deadly Force, in Black and White," *ProPublica*, October 10, 2014, https://www.propublica.org/article/deadly-force-in-black-and-white.

12. Melissa Chan, "Philando Castile Was a Role Model to Hundreds of Kids,

Colleagues Say," *Time*, July 7, 2016, https://time.com/4397086/minne sota-shooting-philando-castile-role-model-school/.

13. "Study Finds Significant Racial Disparities in Homelessness Rates," National Low Income Housing Coalition, April 9, 2018, https://nlihc.org /resource/study-finds-significant-racial-disparities-homelessness-rates.

14. "Five Charts That Explain the Homelessness-Jail Cycle—and How to Break It," Urban Institute, September 16, 2020, https://www.urban.org /features/five-charts-explain-homelessness-jail-cycle-and-how-break-it.

15. Nativeland.ca, accessed August 16, 2021.

16. Joshua Gordon, "Addressing the Crisis of Black Youth Suicide," National Institute of Mental Health, September 22, 2020, https://www.nimh.nih .gov/about/director/messages/2020/addressing-the-crisis-of-black-youth -suicide.

17. Christine Moutier, MD, and Doreen S. Marshall, PhD, "Model School District Policy on Suicide Prevention: Model Language, Commentary, and Resources," Trevor Project, 2019.

bibliography

"Act, Strategies, Caucus and Affinity Groups." Racial Equity Tools. Accessed August 16, 2021. https://www.racialequitytools.org/resources/act/strategies /caucus-and-affinity-groups.

"Appendix A: For Students." Learning for Justice. Accessed August 16, 2021. https://www.learningforjustice.org/magazine/publications/speak-up-at -school/appendices/appendix-a-for-students.

Baptista, Ana Isabel, and Adrienne Perovich. "US Municipal Solid Waste Incinerators: An Industry in Decline." The Tishman Environment and Design Center at The New School, May 2019.

"Basic Requirements." Accessed August 16, 2021. https://www.sba.gov/federal -contracting/contracting-guide/basic-requirements.

"Brands." 15 Percent Pledge. Accessed August 16, 2021. https://www.15percent pledge.org/brands.

Briceño, Norberto. "This Damn Cookie Tin." BuzzFeed, August 31, 2020. https://www.buzzfeed.com/norbertobriceno/growinguphispanic?utm _term=.cpQJZYzl49&sub=4297624_9075238.

Bronson, Po, Beth Allison Barr, Bethany Mandel, and Ashley Merryman. "Even Babies Discriminate: A Nurtureshock Excerpt." Newsweek, January 23, 2014. https://www.newsweek.com/even-babies-discriminate-nurtureshock -excerpt-79233.

Byrd, Ayana. "STUDY: Pennsylvania's Communities of Color in More Danger from Health Consequences of Fracking." Colorlines, July 3, 2018. https:// www.colorlines.com/articles/study-pennsylvanias-communities-color -more-danger-health-consequences-fracking.

Cabrera, Nolan L. "White Immunity: Working Through Some of the Pedagogical Pitfalls of 'Privilege.'" Journal Committed to Social Change on Race and Ethnicity 3, no. 1 (2017): 82.

Chan, Melissa. "Minnesota Shooting: Philando Castile Was Role Model to

Kids." *Time,* July 7, 2016. https://time.com/4397086/minnesota-shooting
-philando-castile-role-model-school/.

Cicchetti, Dante, and John R. Weisz. *Developmental Psychopathology.* Edited by
Suniya S. Luther and Jacob A. Burack. Google Books. Cambridge University Press. Accessed August 16, 2021. https://books.google.com/books?id=
342UddwiAp4C&lpg=PA51&ots=yT4O9K1aDJ&dq=Katz+%26+Kofkin
%2C+1997&lr&pg=PA59#v=onepage&q&f=false.

Coles, Kelly. "Fracking Disproportionately Affects Communities of Color in
Texas, Study Shows." *Texas Monthly,* November 17, 2017. https://www
.texasmonthly.com/news-politics/fracking-disproportionately-affects-com
munities-color-texas-study-shows/.

"Culture." Britannica Kids. Encyclopædia Britannica, Inc. Accessed August 16,
2021. https://kids.britannica.com/kids/article/culture/399913#.

da Costa, Pedro Nicolaci. "The Covid-19 Crisis Has Wiped Out Nearly Half
of Black Small Businesses." *Forbes,* August 28, 2020. https://www.forbes
.com/sites/pedrodacosta/2020/08/10/the-covid-19-crisis-has-wiped
-out-nearly-half-of-black-small-businesses/#:~:text=Nearly%20half%20
of%20Black%20small%20businesses%20had%20been%20wiped%20
out,white%20counterparts%2C%20the%20report%20found.

Elliott, Alicia. "Why Are Parents So Defensive about Play Teepees?" *Today's Parent,* November 28, 2017. https://www.todaysparent.com/family/parenting
/why-are-parents-so-defensive-about-play-teepees/.

Epstein, Rebecca, Thalia Gonzalez, and Jamilia J. Blake. Rep. *Girlhood Interrupted: The Erasure of Black Girls' Childhood.* Washington, DC: Georgetown
Law Center on Poverty and Inequality, n.d.

"Ethane Cracker Plants: What Are They?" Climate Reality, November 6, 2019.
https://www.climaterealityproject.org/blog/ethane-cracker-plants-what
-are-they#:~:text=Ground%2Dlevel%20ozone%2C%20or%20
smog,to%20cancer%20and%20childhood%20leukemia.

"Ethical Consumerism." *Encyclopædia Britannica.* Encyclopædia Britannica, Inc.
Accessed August 16, 2021. https://www.britannica.com/topic/ethical-con
sumerism.

"Five Charts That Explain the Homelessness-Jail Cycle—and How to
Break It." Urban Institute, September 16, 2020. https://www.urban
.org/features/five-charts-explain-homelessness-jail-cycle-and-how
-break-it#:~:text=Homelessness%20and%20the%20criminal%20
justice,loitering%20or%20sleeping%20in%20parks.

Francis, David R. "Employers' Replies to Racial Names." NBER. Accessed August 16, 2021. https://www.nber.org/digest/sep03/employers-replies-racial
-names.

Gabrielson, Ryan, and Eric Sagara. "Deadly Force, in Black and White."

ProPublica. Accessed August 16, 2021. https://www.propublica.org/article
/deadly-force-in-Black-and-white.

"Gender Identity." University of South Dakota. Accessed August 16, 2021.
https://www.usd.edu/diversity-and-inclusiveness/office-for-diversity/safe
-zone-training/gender-identity.

Gerdeman, Dina. "Minorities Who 'Whiten' Job Resumes Get More Inter-
views." HBS Working Knowledge, May 17, 2017. https://hbswk.hbs.edu
/item/minorities-who-whiten-job-resumes-get-more-interviews.

"Good for the Earth, Good for the People." Slow Factory Foundation. Accessed
August 16, 2021. https://slowfactory.foundation/.

Good On You. Accessed August 15, 2021. https://goodonyou.eco/.

Gordon, Joshua. "Addressing the Crisis of Black Youth Suicide." National Institute of Mental Health. US Department of Health and Human Services, September 22, 2020. https://www.nimh.nih.gov/about/director/mes
sages/2020/addressing-the-crisis-of-black-youth-suicide.

Grable, Kaitlin, and Perry Wheeler. "The Plastics Industry Continues to Treat
Black and Brown Lives as Disposable." Greenpeace USA, July 17, 2020.
https://www.greenpeace.org/usa/the-plastics-industry-continues-to-treat
-black-and-brown-lives-as-disposable/.

Grace, Victoria. "Show Up Authentically: Life at the Intersection of Disability
and Multiple Identities." Respect Ability, February 6, 2019. https://www
.respectability.org/2018/09/show-up-and-blend-life-at-the-intersection-of
-disability-and-multiple-identities%E2%80%A8/.

Griffin, Chanté. "How Natural Black Hair at Work Became a Civil Rights Issue."
JSTOR Daily. JSTOR, July 3, 2019. https://daily.jstor.org/how-natural
-black-hair-at-work-became-a-civil-rights-issue/.

Harris, Kamala. "Who Else Keeps Their Spices in Taster's CHOICE Jars?
Turns Out @MindyKaling and I Have More in Common than We Initially Thought. WATCH: HTTPS://T.CO/HQQL2OYB3D PIC.TWIT
TER.COM/9DGQUJKEZF." Twitter, November 26, 2019. https://twit
ter.com/KamalaHarris/status/1199115549705265152?ref_src=twsrc%5E
tfw%7Ctwcamp%5Etweetembed%7Ctwterm%5E11991641576748195
84%7Ctwgr%5E%7Ctwcon%5Es4_&ref_url=https%3A%2F%2Fwww
.balloon-juice.com%2F2019%2F11%2F26%2Fkamala-harris-is-cooking
-again%2F.

Hunter, Margaret. *The Persistent Problem of Colorism: Skin Tone, Status, and Inequality*. Blackwell Publishing, 2007. Reprint.

Intersectional Environmentalist. Accessed August 16, 2021. https://www.inter
sectionalenvironmentalist.com/.

Kelly, David J., Paul C. Quinn, Alan M. Slater, Kang Lee, Alan Gibson, Michael
Smith, Liezhong Ge, and Olivier Pascalis. "Three-Month-Olds, but Not

Newborns, Prefer Own-Race Faces." *Developmental Science*. US National Library of Medicine, November 2005. https://www.ncbi.nlm.nih.gov/pmc/articles/PMC2566511/.

Kiger, Patrick J. "Minimum Wage in America: A Timeline." History.com. A&E Television Networks, October 18, 2019. https://www.history.com/news/minimum-wage-america-timeline.

King, Dr. Martin Luther. "I've Been to the Mountaintop." Transcript. Speeches-USA. Accessed August 16, 2021. http://www.speeches-usa.com/Transcripts/martin_luther_king-mountaintop.html.

Lemish, Dafna, and Colleen Russo Johnson. Reprint. "The Landscape of Children's Television in the US & Canada." The Center for Scholars & Storytellers, 2019.

Love, Dr. Barbara J. "Developing a Liberatory Consciousness." Oregon State University, n.d.

Meyer, Eugene L. "Five Black Men Raided Harpers Ferry with John Brown. They've Been Forgotten." *Washington Post*, October 16, 2019. https://www.washingtonpost.com/history/2019/10/13/five-black-men-raided-harpers-ferry-with-john-brown-theyve-been-forgotten/.

"Minority Communities Need More Parks, Report Says." *Berkeley (CA) Daily Planet*. Accessed August 16, 2021. https://www.berkeleydailyplanet.com/issue/2007-11-13/article/28458?headline=Minority-Communities-Need-More-Parks-Report-Says--By-Angela-Rowen-Special-to-the-Planet.

Morrison, Aaron. "100 Years After Tulsa Race Massacre, the Damage Remains." AP NEWS. Associated Press, May 25, 2021. https://apnews.com/article/tulsa-race-massacre-1921-100-years-later-3bc13e842c31054a90b6d1c81db9d70c.

Morrison, Nick. "Black Students 'Face Racial Bias' in School Discipline." *Forbes*, April 5, 2019. https://www.forbes.com/sites/nickmorrison/2019/04/05/black-students-face-racial-bias-in-school-discipline/?sh=62254be736d5.

Moutier, Christine, and Doreen S. Marshall. "Model School District Policy on Suicide Prevention." The Trevor Project, n.d.

Nativeland.ca. Accessed August 16, 2021. https://native-land.ca/.

News, eBark. "SPS New Inclusive Dress Policy." Garfield High School PTSA, October 8, 2019. https://garfieldptsa.org/sps-new-inclusive-dress-policy.

Okun, Tema. "White Supremacy Culture." https://www.dismantlingracism.org/.

Oluo, Ijeoma. Essay. In *So You Want to Talk about Race*, 28. New York: Seal Press, 2020.

Perry, Andre. "Racist Dress Codes in Schools Are the New 'Whites Only' Signs." Hechinger Report, March 30, 2020. https://hechingerreport.org/dress-codes-are-the-new-whites-only-signs/.

"Racial Bias May Begin in Babies at Six Months, U of T Research Reveals."

University of Toronto News. Accessed August 16, 2021. https://www.uto
ronto.ca/news/racial-bias-may-begin-babies-six-months-u-t-research-re
veals.

Rogers, Fred. *The World According to Mister Rogers: Important Things to Remember*. London: Hachette Books, 2019.

Sikes, Chloe Latham. "Racial and Gender Disparities in Dress Code Discipline Point to Need for New Approaches in Schools." IDRA. The Intercultural Development Research Association, February 2020. https://www.idra.org/resource-center/racial-and-gender-disparities-in-dress-code-discipline-point-to-need-for-new-approaches-in-schools/.

Singleton, Glenn E., and James P. Comer. *More Courageous Conversations about Race*. Amazon. Corwin Press, 2013.

"Species." Merriam-Webster.com. Accessed August 17, 2021. https://www.merriam-webster.com/dictionary/species.

Specter, Emma. "'Emotional Labor' Is Not What You Think It Is." *Vogue*, November 20, 2019. https://www.vogue.com/article/what-is-emotional-labor.

"Study Finds Significant Racial Disparities in Homelessness Rates." National Low Income Housing Coalition, April 9, 2018. https://nlihc.org/resource/study-finds-significant-racial-disparities-homelessness-rates.

Teaching Tolerance. "Hate at School: 2018 Teacher Comments." Southern Poverty Law Center, n.d.

Walker, Alice. *In Search of Our Mothers' Gardens: Womanist Prose*. San Diego: Harcourt Brace Jovanovich, 1983. https://archive.org/details/insearchof
ourmot00walk.

Weber, Sam, and Connie Kargbo. "Black Families Increasingly Choose to Homeschool Kids." PBS. Public Broadcasting Service, April 22, 2018. https://www.pbs.org/newshour/show/black-families-increasingly-choose-to-home
school-kids.

"Wee the People: About." weethepeople.com. Accessed August 16, 2021. https://www.weethepeopleboston.org/about.

Wellman, David T. *Portraits of White Racism*. Cambridge, MA: Cambridge University Press, 1994.

"Where to Buy Fair Trade Chocolate." Fair Trade Certified. Accessed August 16, 2021. https://www.fairtradecertified.org/shopping-guides/fair-trade-chocol
ate?gclid=Cj0KCQjw78yFBhCZARIsAOxgSx27x4TlLMqEo41jRKd0A6
3X8tOgNjsJqLWkIvTaUpdmnaXE4IslcS4aAvw4EALw_wcB.

"White Antiracism in US History." Cross Cultural Solidarity History Project, May 10, 2021. https://crossculturalsolidarity.com/white-antiracism-in-u-s
-history/.

Wolcott, Victoria W. "The Forgotten History of Segregated Swimming Pools and Amusement Parks." *Conversation*, July 27, 2021. https://theconversation

.com/the-forgotten-history-of-segregated-swimming-pools-and-amuse
ment-parks-119586.

Wong, Brittany. "Why White People Are Bad at Interracial Friendships (and
How to Do Better)." *HuffPost*, September 5, 2020. https://www.huffpost
.com/entry/close-interracial-friendships_l_5f5122c8c5b6946f3eaed704.

index

ABAR (anti-biased and antiracist) parenting, xi, 4. *See also* antiracism
ableism, 34, 62, 223
accomplice(s), 10–11, 37
accountability, 5, 160
  as antiracist value, 123
  compassionate, 214–16
  conversation agreements and, 13–14
  in order to be a co-conspirator, 33
accountability/allyship stage, when building a liberatory community, 201
action stage, for building a liberatory community, 201
activities
  for building a relationship, 216–17
  building a school, 76–77
  critical review of media, 138–39
  curating an antiracist book collection, 147–48
  emailing companies lacking racial justice consciousness, 192–93
  How Diverse Is Your Universe, 262–63
  land acknowledgment, 240–41
  making an affirmative song playlist, 80
  making lists of locally owned and PoGM-owned businesses, 186–87
  painting handprints, 91
  self-portraits, 83
adolescents. *See also* ten- to thirteen-year-olds
  antiracism awareness for, 49–50
  choosing guidelines for media, 137
  colorism and, 51, 52
  consent and, 14–15
  Cultures Are Not Costumes Checklist for, 191

email template for companies lacking racial justice consciousness, 192–93
learning by, 47–48
making lists of locally owned and PoGM-owned businesses to support, 186–87
adults. *See also* parents (caregivers) and parenting partners; teachers
  fear of conflict manifested in, 118
  perfectionism manifested in, 114
  power hoarding manifesting in, 116
advocacy
  for a friend who just experienced racism, 205–8
  to include Black people in school curriculum, 244–45
  when someone is misgendered, 212
advocacy phrases, 15
affinity effect (in-group bias), 11, 12
affinity spaces, 199–200, 223
affinity spaces of color, 200
Afro-Latine/x peoples, 18, 51
Alaska Natives, 18
ally(ies), 10, 11
  moving to being a co-conspirator from being an, 32–38
  moving to being an accomplice from being an, 32
  role of, 31–32
  roles of, in Pyramid of Accountability, 36
Amazon (website), 185
analyze stage, for building a liberatory community, 201
Anderson, Osborne, 121
Andrews, Dorinda J. Carter, 70
Anti-Asian violence, 164

about the authors

Britt Hawthorne (she/they) is a Black biracial momma, teacher, author, and anti-bias and antiracist facilitator. Britt partners with caregivers, educators, and families to raise the next generation of antiracist children. Together with her beloved partner, she is raising her children to become empathic, critical thinkers, embracing justice and activism. Her days are filled with coffee, teaching, and joy. To learn more, visit britthawthorne.com.

Natasha Yglesias (she/her) is a queer Latina writer and editor based in Northern California, specifically on the unceded territory of the Muwekma Ohlone Tribe in the Bay Area. She's a fiction graduate of the Bennington Writing Seminars and a submissions reader for several literary magazines. Natasha is committed to centering people of the global majority and fostering equitable environments for present and future generations of all ages and backgrounds. To view her previously published work, you can visit natashayglesias.com. To engage in conversation, follow her on Twitter: @TashaYglesias.